KT-439-519

Contents

Introduction   IV

Map   VI

Story   1

Character list   101

Cultural notes   102

Glossary   105

✦ INTRODUCTION ✦

ABOUT COLLINS ENGLISH READERS

Collins English Readers have been created for readers worldwide whose first language is not English. The stories are carefully graded to ensure that you, the reader, will both enjoy and benefit from your reading experience.

Words which are above the required reading level are underlined the first time they appear in a story. All underlined words are defined in the **Glossary** at the back of the book. Books at levels 1 and 2 take their definitions from the *Collins COBUILD Essential English Dictionary*, and books at levels 3 and above from the *Collins COBUILD Advanced Learner's Dictionary*. Where appropriate, definitions are simplified for level and context.

Alongside the glossary, a **Character list** is provided to help the reader identify who is who, and how they are connected to each other. **Cultural notes** explain historical, cultural and other references. **Maps and diagrams** are provided where appropriate.

To support both teachers and learners, additional materials are available online at www.collins.co.uk/pages/elt-english-readers. These include a **plot synopsis** and a **level checker**.

 You can **download the audio** of the full story at www.collins.co.uk/pages/elt-english-readers-elt-readers-audio-resources.

About Agatha Christie

Agatha Christie (1890–1976) is known throughout the world as the Queen of Crime. She is the most widely published and translated author of all time and in any language; only the Bible and Shakespeare have sold more copies.

Agatha Christie's first novel was published in 1920. It featured Hercule Poirot, the Belgian detective who has become the most popular detective in crime fiction since Sherlock Holmes.

Collins has published Agatha Christie since 1926.

The Grading Scheme

The Collins COBUILD Grading Scheme has been created using the most up-to-date language usage information available today. Each level is guided by a comprehensive grammar and vocabulary framework, ensuring that the series will perfectly match readers' abilities.

		CEF band	Pages	Word count	Headwords
Level 1	elementary	A2	64	5,000–8,000	approx. 700
Level 2	pre-intermediate	A2–B1	80	8,000–11,000	approx. 900
Level 3	intermediate	B1	96	11,000–20,000	approx. 1,300
Level 4	upper-intermediate	B2	112-128	15,000–26,000	approx. 1,700
Level 5	upper-intermediate+	B2+	128+	22,000–30,000	approx. 2,200
Level 6	advanced	C1	144+	28,000+	2,500+
Level 7	advanced+	C2	160+	varied	varied

For more information on the Collins COBUILD Grading Scheme go to www.collins.co.uk/pages/elt-english-readers-collins-cobuild-grading-scheme.

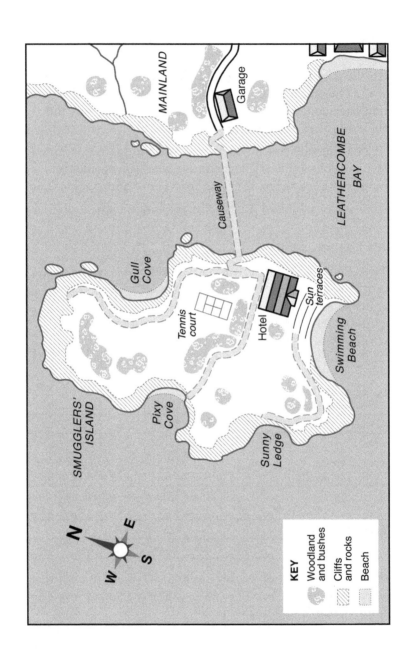

CHAPTER I

Hercule Poirot, who was looking very fine in a white suit with a <u>panama hat</u> over his eyes – his moustache as magnificent as usual – relaxed in a <u>deck chair</u> and looked at the beach. Steps led down to it from the terrace of the Jolly Roger Hotel. There were people swimming in the sea, and others sunbathing on the sand.

On Poirot's left, Mrs Carrie Gardener talked gently and without stopping, in a pleasant American accent, while her <u>knitting needles</u> made a constant 'clack clack' sound. On her other side, her husband, Odell Gardener, replied briefly when he felt it was absolutely necessary.

On Poirot's right, Miss Emily Brewster, a strong athletic woman with very curly hair, made a few comments in a <u>gruff</u> voice.

Mrs Gardener was saying, 'And so I said to Mr Gardener, sightseeing is all very well. But we've seen everything in England, and all I want now is to relax by the seaside. That's what I said, wasn't it, Odell? Just relax.'

Mr Gardener <u>murmured</u>, 'Yes, darling.'

'So I mentioned it to Mr Kelso, at Cook's Travel Agency – and he arranged everything for us and has been most helpful. Well, Mr Kelso said we couldn't do better than to come to the coast of Devon[1], and to stay on <u>Smugglers'</u> Island[2]. A beautiful place just off Leathercombe Bay, he said, and very comfortable and exclusive with sun terraces and a tennis court. And the most interesting people come here – and I see he was right. Oh, I was just so excited when I found out who you were, wasn't I, Odell?'

'You were, darling.'

'You see, Monsieur Poirot, I'd heard a lot about you from Cornelia Robson, when we saw her at Badenhof. Cornelia told us all about that <u>business</u> in Egypt when Linnet Ridgeway was killed. She said you were wonderful and I've always been desperate to meet you, haven't I, Odell?'

'Yes, darling.'

'And then there's Miss Darnley, of whom I am a *huge* fan. I buy a lot of my things at Rose Mond's and of course she *is* Rose Mond – she does all the designing for the brand herself, you know. I think her clothes are marvellous. That dress I was wearing last night was one of hers. She's a lovely woman.'

From the other side of Miss Brewster, Major[3] Barry grunted, 'Very lovely-looking girl!'

Mrs Gardener clacked her knitting needles.

'I've just got to admit one thing, Monsieur Poirot. It shocked me meeting you here – not that I wasn't thrilled. But I did think that you might be here – well, professionally. I'm terribly sensitive, as Mr Gardener will tell you, and I just couldn't bear to be involved in some sort of crime.'

'Let me assure you, madame, I am simply here for a holiday. I am not even thinking about crime,' said Poirot.

Miss Brewster said, in her gruff voice, 'There are no dead bodies on Smugglers' Island.'

'Ah! But you could be forgiven for thinking that were not true.' Poirot pointed down to the beach: 'Look at the sunbathers – there is nothing individual about them. All they wish to do is get a suntan. They barely move. *Bah*, who can tell them apart? They lie in rows, so still that they might be <u>corpses</u>!'

'Monsieur Poirot!' Mrs Gardener was shocked.

'Perhaps I have gone too far,' Poirot admitted.

'Still,' Mrs Gardener <u>knitted</u> with energy, 'I do agree with you on one point, Monsieur Poirot. These girls that lie out like that in the sun are making a big mistake. It's not good for you.

I've said so to Irene — that's my daughter, Monsieur Poirot. Irene, I said to her, lying out in the sun like that is bad for the skin. I said that to her, didn't I, Odell?'

'Yes, darling.'

Mrs Gardener rolled up her <u>knitting</u> and said, 'Odell, shall we go up for coffee now?'

'Yes, darling.'

Mr Gardener struggled out of his chair and picked up Mrs Gardener's knitting and her book. The Gardeners went up to the hotel.

Miss Brewster said, 'American husbands are wonderful!'

◆

Mrs Gardener's place was taken by Stephen Lane, a tall, energetic man of about fifty. He said with enthusiasm, 'Marvellous countryside! I've been to Harford and back over the cliffs today.'

'It's very hot for walking, isn't it?' said Major Barry, who never walked anywhere.

'Walking is good exercise,' said Miss Brewster. 'I haven't been out for my usual row yet today, but there's nothing as good as rowing for your stomach muscles.'

Hercule Poirot's eyes looked down at his round middle.

Miss Brewster said kindly, 'You'd soon get rid of that, Monsieur Poirot, if you took a rowing boat out every day.'

'*Merci* – thank you, mademoiselle... but I hate boats! The movement of the sea is not pleasant.'

'<u>Seasickness</u> is odd,' said Miss Brewster. 'Why should some people get it and not others? And it's nothing to do with our ordinary health. Then there's the way some people don't like heights. I'm not very good with heights myself, but Mrs Redfern is far worse. The other day, on the cliff path to Harford, she felt quite unwell and had to hold on to me. She told me she once got stuck going down those outside stairs on Milan Cathedral. She'd gone up without any problems but felt ill coming back down.'

'She'd better not go down the ladder to Pixy <u>Cove</u>[2], then,' observed Lane.

Miss Brewster said sadly, 'I can't do that myself either.'

Lane said, 'Here's Mrs Redfern now, coming back from her swim.'

Miss Brewster remarked, 'Monsieur Poirot should approve of her. She's no sunbather.'

Young Mrs Redfern had taken off her swimming cap and was shaking out her hair. She was a blonde and her skin was very pale.

Major Barry laughed and said, 'She looks a bit "uncooked" among the others, doesn't she?'

Wrapping herself in a long <u>bathrobe</u>, Christine Redfern came up the steps towards them. She had a serious face and small, delicate hands and feet. She smiled and sat down beside them.

Miss Brewster said, 'You've earned Monsieur Poirot's good opinion. He doesn't like the suntanning crowd.'

Christine Redfern smiled sadly.

'I wish I could sunbathe! But I don't go brown – I only burn.'

Emily Brewster said, 'Monsieur Poirot says the sunbathers look like corpses.' She turned to Poirot: 'You know, I wish you had told Mrs Gardener that you *were* here investigating a really horrible murder, and that you believed the murderer was definitely one of the guests.'

Poirot sighed. 'I very much fear she would have believed me,' he said.

Major Barry laughed: 'She certainly would have.'

Emily Brewster said, 'No, I don't believe even Mrs Gardener would have believed in a crime here. This isn't the sort of place you'd find a corpse!'

Poirot protested, 'But why not, mademoiselle? Why should there not be a killing here?'

Emily Brewster said, 'I suppose some places are more unlikely than others. This isn't that kind of place.'

'It is peaceful, yes,' agreed Poirot. 'The sun shines. The sea is blue. But you forget, Miss Brewster, that there is evil everywhere under the sun.'

Stephen Lane leaned forward. His blue eyes lit up.

'Oh, yes indeed, Monsieur Poirot! It is a terrible truth that many people have hearts that are full of evil. Nowadays, no one believes in evil. Evil, people say, is done by those who know no better – who should be pitied rather than blamed, but Monsieur Poirot, evil is real! It exists! It is powerful! It walks the earth!'

He stopped. His breathing was fast. He wiped his forehead with his handkerchief.

'I'm sorry. I got carried away.'

Major Barry coughed. 'Evil, eh...? Do you know, when I was in India—'

Major Barry had been at the Jolly Roger for long enough for everyone to recognise when he was starting on one of his long Indian stories. Both Miss Brewster and Mrs Redfern burst into speech.

'That's your husband swimming in now, isn't it, Mrs Redfern?'

'Oh look! What a lovely little boat out there. It's Mr Blatt's, isn't it?'

And the story about India was successfully avoided.

Poirot looked at the young man who had just swum to shore. Patrick Redfern was slim and suntanned. He had broad shoulders and a manner that made him popular with all women and most men.

He waved to his wife.

She waved back, calling out, 'Come up here, Pat.'

'I'm coming.'

Patrick went along the beach to get his towel.

It was then that a woman came past them from the hotel.

Her arrival was like a stage entrance and she walked as though she knew it. She was used to the effect her presence produced.

She was tall, thin and suntanned. She was wearing a simple white swimsuit and was as perfect as a statue. Her hair was a red-brown colour and it curled perfectly around her face. Although you could see from her face that she must be over thirty, the overall effect was of youth, superb and full of life. On her head she wore a stylish sun hat made of green cardboard.

She made every other woman on the beach seem unimportant. And every man present was watching her.

Stephen Lane drew in his breath with a little <u>hiss</u>.

Major Barry said in a whisper, 'Arlena Stuart, that's who she was before she left the stage. She's worth looking at, eh?'

Christine Redfern's voice was cold: 'She's beautiful, yes. But I think she looks unkind!'

Emily Brewster said suddenly, 'You talked about evil, Monsieur Poirot. Now if you ask me, that woman is evil! I happen to know a good deal about her.'

Major Barry said, 'I remember a girl out in Simla, in India. She had red hair too. Men went mad about her! The women, of course, would have liked to pull her eyes out!'

Stephen Lane said with extreme feeling, 'Such women are dangerous.'

Arlena Stuart had reached the water's edge. Two young men had sprung up and come eagerly towards her. She smiled at them, but her eyes slid past them to Patrick Redfern.

It was, Poirot thought, like watching the needle of a compass. Patrick Redfern's feet changed their direction and brought him to Arlena Stuart.

Arlena moved slowly away along the beach – Patrick went with her. Then she stretched herself out by a rock. Patrick dropped to the sand beside her.

Christine Redfern got up and went into the hotel.

Emily Brewster said, 'It's too bad – Christine's a nice little thing. They've only been married a year or two. Patrick Redfern's a fool!'

Hercule Poirot said nothing. He was gazing down the beach, but not at Patrick Redfern and Arlena Stuart.

Miss Brewster said, 'Well, I'd better go and get my boat.' She left them.

Major Barry turned his pale green eyes on Poirot.

'Well,' he said. 'What do you think of the <u>siren</u>?' Then he asked with sudden curiosity, 'And what are you looking at?'

Hercule Poirot replied, 'At the one man who did not look up when she passed.'

Major Barry followed Poirot's gaze to a man of about forty, with fair hair and a suntan. He had a quiet, pleasant face and sat smoking a <u>pipe</u> and reading *The Times*.

'Oh!' said Major Barry. 'That's her husband – that's Marshall.'

Poirot said, 'Yes, I know.'

Major Barry said, 'He seems a nice man. Quiet. I wonder if my *Times* has come.'

He got up and went towards the hotel.

Poirot's glance turned to Stephen Lane, who was watching Arlena Marshall and Patrick Redfern. Lane turned suddenly to Poirot: 'That woman is completely evil. Don't you agree?'

Poirot said, 'It is difficult to be sure.'

Stephen Lane said, 'But don't you feel it in the air? All round you? The presence of evil?'

Slowly, Hercule Poirot nodded.

CHAPTER 2

When Rosamund Darnley sat down by him, Hercule Poirot did not hide his pleasure.

He admired Rosamund as much as any woman he had ever met. He liked her sophisticated manner, the attractive lines of her figure, the way she held her head. He liked her smooth, shiny dark hair and her amused smile. She was wearing a navy blue dress with white flashes on it. It looked very simple and very expensive. As Mrs Gardener had said, Rosamund Darnley, as Rose Mond Ltd, was one of London's best-known dress designers.

She said, 'I don't think I like this place. I'm wondering why I came here!'

Poirot answered gently, 'Has something happened to worry you?'

She nodded. Her foot swung back and forwards. She stared down at it. 'I've met a ghost.'

'A ghost, mademoiselle? The ghost of what? Or of whom?'

'Oh, the ghost of myself.'

Poirot asked gently, 'Was it a painful ghost?'

'Unexpectedly painful. It took me back, you know...' She paused, thinking. Then she said, 'Imagine my childhood. No, you can't! You're not English!'

Poirot asked, 'Was it a very English childhood?'

'Oh, incredibly so! The country, a big old house, horses, dogs, walks in the rain, apples in the orchard, a lack of money...'

Poirot asked gently, 'And you want to go back? To your childhood?'

Rosamund shook her head.

'You can't go back. Ever. But I'd like to have moved forward in a different way.'

Poirot said, 'When I was young, there was a game called, "If you were not yourself, who would you be?" The answer, mademoiselle, is not very easy to find.'

Rosamund said, 'No, I suppose not. It could be a big risk. You wouldn't like to take on being Mussolini[4] or Princess Elizabeth[5]. As for your friends, you know too much about them.'

After a moment Poirot said, 'Many people, mademoiselle, must envy you.'

She thought about it, her lips curved in their amused smile.

'Yes, I'm the perfect successful woman! The successful creative artist and the successful businesswoman. I'm very rich, I've got a good figure, quite a nice face, and I don't gossip too much about other people.'

She paused. Her smile widened.

'Of course, I haven't got a husband! I've failed there, haven't I, Monsieur Poirot?'

Poirot said politely, 'Mademoiselle, if you are not married, it is by choice.'

Rosamund said, 'And yet, like all men, I'm sure you believe that no woman is content unless she is married and has children.'

Poirot said, 'To marry and have children is the common experience of most women[6]. But only one woman in a thousand can be as successful and well-known as you are.'

Rosamund smiled broadly at him.

'And yet, all the same, I'm nothing but an unhappy <u>old maid</u>! That's what I feel today. I'd be happier with two pence a year, a big silent husband and lots of annoying children running after me. That's true, isn't it?'

'If you say so, mademoiselle.'

Rosamund laughed. She was in a good mood once again.

'Thank you, Monsieur Poirot. Of course, I'm lucky as I am – and I know it!'

Poirot murmured, 'So, Captain[3] Marshall is an old friend of yours, mademoiselle?'

Rosamund sat up.

'How did you know that? Oh, I suppose Ken told you.'

Poirot shook his head.

'Nobody told me. After all, mademoiselle, I am a detective. It was obvious.'

'I don't see how,' Rosamund said.

'But think about it!' Poirot moved his hands as he spoke. 'You have been here a week. In that time, you are lively, happy, without a care. Today, suddenly, you speak of ghosts, of old times. What has changed? There have been no new arrivals until last night when Captain Marshall and his wife and daughter arrived. Today, there is a change in you! It is obvious!'

Rosamund said, 'Well, it's true. Kenneth Marshall and I were children together. The Marshalls lived next door. Ken was always nice to me, though he was four years older. I haven't seen him for a long time. It must be – fifteen years at least.'

Poirot said thoughtfully, 'That is a long time.'

Rosamund nodded. She said, 'Ken's so sweet. One of the best. Very quiet. His only fault is making unfortunate marriages. He's a complete fool where women are concerned! Do you remember the Martingdale case?'

Poirot thought.

'Martingdale? It was <u>arsenic</u>, wasn't it?'

'Yes. Seventeen or eighteen years ago. The woman was <u>tried</u> for the murder of her husband,' said Rosamund.

'And he was proved to have been an arsenic user and she was acquitted?' asked Poirot.

'That's right. Well, after the trial, Ken married her. That's the sort of silly thing he does.'

Poirot murmured, 'But if she was innocent?'

Rosamund said impatiently, 'Oh, I'm sure she was innocent. Nobody really knows! But there are plenty of women to marry in the world without going out of your way to marry one who's stood trial for murder.'

Poirot said nothing.

'He was very young, of course, only twenty-one. He was mad about her. She died when Linda was born – a year after their marriage.'

She paused.

'And then came Arlena Stuart. She was an actress at the time, and had just been mixed up in the Codrington divorce case. Lady⁷ Codrington divorced her husband, citing Arlena Stuart. They said Lord⁷ Codrington was totally in love with her. They were supposed to be married as soon as the divorce was final. But he didn't marry her. I believe she actually sued him for breach of promise. It was big news at the time.

'Anyway, the next thing that happens is that Ken marries her. The fool!'

Poirot murmured, 'She is very beautiful, mademoiselle.'

'Yes, there's no doubt of that. But then there was another scandal about three years ago. Old Sir⁷ Roger Erskine died and left her all his money. Well, I would have thought that would have made Ken walk away.'

'And did it not?' asked Poirot.

'Apparently not. I told you, I haven't seen him for years. People say, though, that he was completely calm about it. I'd like to know why. Has he got an absolutely <u>blind belief</u> in her?'

'There might be other reasons,' suggested Poirot gently.

'Yes,' agreed Rosamund. 'Pride, perhaps. Oh, I don't know what he really feels about her. Nobody does.'

'And her? What does she feel about him?'

Rosamund stared at him.

'She's a <u>gold-digger</u>. A <u>man-eater</u> as well! If anything attractive in trousers comes close to her, it's a fresh opportunity for a bit of fun for Arlena! She's that kind of person.'

'Yes,' Poirot said. 'That is true. Her eyes look for only one thing – men.'

Rosamund continued: 'She's got her eye on Patrick Redfern now. He's very fond of his wife – but that's just the kind of man Arlena likes. I like little Mrs Redfern. She's pretty in her fair pale way. She was a school teacher, I believe. She's the kind of person who thinks that <u>mind is stronger than matter</u>. Well, she's got a shock coming to her. I don't think she'll stand a chance against that man-eating tiger, Arlena.'

Rosamund got up. 'It's a shame, you know.'

Then she added, 'Somebody should do something about it.'

◆ ◆ ◆

Linda Marshall was examining her face in her bedroom mirror. She disliked her face very much. She also disliked her heavy bush of soft brown hair, her green-grey eyes and the long, angry line of her chin.

'It's awful being sixteen,' she said to her reflection.

She felt <u>awkward</u>. She knew that she was big and clumsy. And she knew that she didn't want to live at home any longer.

Arlena...

Oh, how very much she disliked her stepmother.

'She's horrible!'

Not that Arlena was unkind. Most of the time she hardly noticed Linda. But when she did, Linda felt that Arlena was laughing at her. And Arlena was so beautiful and perfect that it made Linda feel even less perfect in comparison.

But it wasn't only that. No, it was something that Arlena did to people – to Father.

'She's bad,' thought Linda. 'Bad!'

Father was quite different when he was with Arlena. He was all... all sort of bottled up and not... not there.

Linda thought, 'And it'll go on like this, month after month. I can't bear it.'

Hate of Arlena suddenly filled her mind. She thought, 'I'd like to kill her. Oh! I do wish she'd die!'

She looked out of the window to the sea below.

'This place could be fun,' Linda thought, 'if only Arlena would go away.'

It had been exciting coming across to the island from the mainland[2]. The tide had been up over the causeway, so they had come by boat. The hotel had looked exciting, and unusual. And then on the terrace, a tall dark-haired woman had jumped up and said, 'Kenneth?'

And her father had been surprised: 'Rosamund!'

Linda approved of Rosamund Darnley. Rosamund was sensible. And she had a kind of funny, amused face – as though it were amused at herself, not at you. Rosamund had been nice to her – she hadn't looked as though she thought Linda was a fool. In fact, she'd treated Linda as though she was a real human being.

Father had seemed pleased to see Rosamund, too.

Funny – he'd looked quite different, all of a sudden. He'd looked... young, that was it! He'd laughed. Now Linda came to think about it, she hadn't heard him laugh very often recently. It was as though he was someone quite different at that moment.

But you couldn't enjoy yourself with Arlena nearby. You couldn't be happy when there was a person there you hated. Yes, hated. She hated Arlena.

◆ ◆ ◆

When you came out of the hotel on the south side, the terraces and the swimming beach were below you. There was also a path that led off round the cliff on the south-west side of the island. A little way along it, a few steps led down to a series of seats cut into the cliff, labelled on the hotel map as Sunny <u>Ledge</u>[2].

This was where Patrick Redfern and his wife came immediately after dinner. It was a lovely clear night with a bright moon.

The Redferns sat down on one of the benches overlooking the bay. For a while they were silent. At last Patrick Redfern said, 'It's a beautiful evening, isn't it, Christine?'

Christine Redfern asked in her quiet voice, 'Did you know that woman was going to be here?'

He turned towards her quickly.

'I don't know what's wrong with you—'

She interrupted. Her voice trembled. 'Wrong with *me*? It's what's wrong with *you*! Oh, Patrick! I wanted to go to Tintagel again – where we had our honeymoon. But you insisted on coming here. Was it because *she* was going to be here? You're in love with her, aren't you?'

'Christine, don't make a fool of yourself!' said Patrick. 'We won't go on being happy if I can't even speak to another woman without you getting all upset.'

'Oh, it's not like that.'

'Yes, it is. In marriage, people have… well… friendships with other people. This suspicious attitude is all wrong, Christine. Don't get jealous of every pretty woman we meet.'

Christine said, 'She's not just any pretty woman! She's… she's different! She's a bad person! She'll do you harm. Patrick, please. Let's get away from here.'

'Don't be ridiculous, Christine. And let's not argue about it. Come on, let's go back to the hotel.'

He got up. There was a pause, then Christine got up, too.

On a nearby seat, Hercule Poirot sat and shook his head sadly.

CHAPTER 3

Rosamund Darnley and Kenneth Marshall sat on the cliff overlooking Gull Cove. This was on the east side of the island. People came here in the morning sometimes to swim.

'You haven't changed much, Rosamund,' Marshall said. 'You're very successful and you're rich, but you're the same Rosamund.'

Rosamund murmured, 'I wish I were. But I've changed so much. It's a pity, isn't it, Kenneth, that we can't keep the nice natures and high ideals that we had when we were young?'

'I don't know that your nature was ever particularly nice, my dear. You used to get into the most unpleasant rages. You nearly killed me once when you flew at me in a temper.'

Rosamund laughed.

Then came a pause.

Rosamund said at last, 'Kenneth? If I say something that's probably very rude, will you never speak to me again?'

'I don't think,' he said seriously, 'that I would ever regard anything you said as very rude. 'You see, from when we were children together, I've always been so perfectly happy with you.'

Rosamund nodded, understanding all that last phrase meant. But she did not show him the pleasure that it gave her.

'Kenneth, why don't you get a divorce?' she asked.

His face changed. The happy expression died. He said quietly, 'You don't understand.'

'Are you really so fond of her?'

'It's not a question of that. You see, I married her.'

'I know. But she's— notorious.'

Kenneth considered that for a moment.

'I suppose she is.'

'You *could* divorce her, Ken. Or you could make her divorce you – if you prefer it that way.'

'Yes. I'm sure I could.'

'You should, Ken. Think of your daughter. Arlena's not good for Linda.'

Kenneth said, 'Yes. I know.'

'I like Linda,' Rosamund continued. 'Very much. There's something lovely about her. I think she feels things deeply.'

Kenneth said, 'She's like her mother. She finds some things difficult, like Ruth did.'

'Then don't you think you should <u>get rid of</u> Arlena?'

'A divorce?'

'Yes. People are doing it all the time now.'

Kenneth said, 'Yes, and that's what I hate.'

'Hate?' She was surprised.

'Yes. The sort of attitude to life there is nowadays. If you say you'll do something and then you don't like it, then you get yourself out of it as quickly as possible! Well, I think it's wrong. If you marry a woman and promise to look after her, well, it's up to you to do that. I'm sick of quick marriage and easy divorce. Arlena's my wife and that's all there is to it.'

Rosamund leaned forward. She said in a low voice, 'So it's like that with you? "Till death do us part"[8]?'

Kenneth nodded.

◆ ◆ ◆

Hercule Poirot and Horace Blatt were enjoying a drink.

Blatt said, 'So you're the famous detective, eh?'

Poirot accepted the remark with his usual lack of <u>modesty</u>.

Blatt was a large man with a red face and a circle of brown hair around a shiny bald spot on the top of his head. It seemed that it was his ambition to be the <u>life and soul</u> of any place he happened to be in. The Jolly Roger Hotel, in his opinion (which he shared loudly) needed brightening up – and so he was puzzled at the way people seemed to disappear whenever he arrived somewhere.

Blatt went on, 'And what are you doing down here? Are you on a job?'

'No, no. I am resting. I am taking a holiday.'

Blatt <u>winked</u>. 'You'd say that anyway, wouldn't you?'

Poirot asked, 'And why would you think that?'

'Oh, a man like you would go on holiday somewhere far more exotic and grand than this little corner of Devon.'

Poirot sighed. He looked out of the window. Rain was falling, and there was mist over the island. 'It is possible that you are right!' he said.

'I don't really know why I came here either,' Blatt continued. 'I think it was the name. The Jolly Roger Hotel, Smugglers' Island – it made me think of when I was a boy. Pirates, <u>smuggling</u>, all that.'

He laughed at himself.

'I used to sail a bit as a boy. A taste for that sort of thing never leaves you. I like going out in that little boat of mine. Redfern's keen on sailing, too, you know. He's been out with me once or twice.'

He broke off, as the subject of his words came into the bar.

'Hello, Redfern. What will you have to drink? What about you, Monsieur Poirot?' asked Blatt.

Poirot shook his head.

Patrick Redfern sat down and said, 'Were you talking about sailing? It's the best fun in the world. I wish I could do more of it. I used to spend most of my time as a boy in a tiny boat, sailing round this coast.'

Poirot said, 'Then you know this part of the world well?'

'Oh yes! I knew this place before it was a hotel. It was an old house. It hadn't been lived in for years. There used to be all sorts of stories of secret passages from the house to Pixy's Cave.'

Blatt spilt his drink. He asked, 'What is this Pixy's Cave?'

Redfern said, 'Oh, don't you know it? It's at Pixy Cove. It's quite hard to find the entrance. It's hidden behind a big pile of rocks at one end. It's just a long thin gap. You can just squeeze through. Inside it widens out into quite a big cave though. You can imagine how much fun it was to go inside as a boy!'

Poirot said, 'But what is this "Pixy"?'

'Oh, that's typical of Devon,' Redfern said. 'A pixy is a tiny <u>imaginary</u>, magical creature. There's the famous pixy's cave at Sheepstor.'

Blatt looked at his watch.

'Well, I'm going in to dinner. On the whole, Redfern, I prefer pirates to pixies.'

As Blatt went out, Poirot said, 'Monsieur Blatt is an interesting character.'

'I don't know much about him,' said Redfern. 'I've been sailing with him once or twice – but he doesn't really like having anyone with him. He prefers to be on his own.'

'That is strange,' said Poirot. 'It is very different to how he is on land.'

◆ ◆ ◆

Hercule Poirot paused in the hall after dinner. The doors were open and the soft night air was coming in. The rain had stopped, and the mist had gone. It was a fine night again.

Poirot walked out and towards the edge of the cliff. A few minutes later, he followed the winding path back to the hotel. He was nearly there when he heard voices. There was a gap in the bushes.

He saw Arlena Marshall and Patrick Redfern talking. The man's voice was full of emotion. 'I'm crazy about you – you know I am. Tell me that you do care about me. Just a little?'

Poirot saw Arlena Marshall's face. He thought it was like a happy cat. She said softly, 'Of course, Patrick darling, I <u>adore</u> you…'

Poirot continued walking along the path. A figure joined him suddenly. It was Captain Marshall.

'Perfect night, isn't it?' he said. 'After that awful weather today.' Marshall looked up at the sky: 'We should have fine weather tomorrow.'

CHAPTER 4

The morning of 25 August was bright and there were no clouds in the sky.

It was eight o'clock when Linda put down her book and looked in the mirror. Her lips were closed tightly together.

She said firmly to her reflection, *'I'm going to do it.'*

She slipped into her swimsuit, then put on a bathrobe and beach shoes. She went out of her room and along the corridor. From there, a door led to outside stairs which went down to the rocks below the hotel. The stairs were used by hotel guests for a quick before-breakfast swim, instead of going down to the main swimming beach.

As Linda made her way down the stairs, she met her father coming up.

'You're up early. Are you going for a swim?' he asked.

Linda nodded.

♦ ◆ ♦

Christine Redfern was standing in Linda's room when the girl returned.

'Oh, there you are,' Christine said. 'I didn't think you'd be up yet.'

'I've been swimming,' Linda said.

Noticing the parcel in Linda's hand, Christine said with surprise, 'The post has come early today.'

Linda's face turned red. In her usual nervous, clumsy way, the parcel slipped from her hand and the contents rolled over the floor.

'Oh!' Christine said in a surprised voice. 'What have you been buying candles for?'

But to Linda's relief, Christine did not wait for an answer. As she helped to pick up the candles, she said, 'Anyway, I came in to ask whether you'd like to come with me to Gull Cove this morning. I want to draw there.'

Linda accepted eagerly.

In the last few days she had often accompanied Christine Redfern on drawing expeditions. She thought perhaps Christine found the excuse of painting a help to her pride, since her husband now spent most of his time with Arlena Marshall.

Linda liked being with Christine, who spoke very little. There was a kind of sympathy between them, probably based on their dislike of the same person.

Christine said, 'I'm playing tennis at twelve, so we'd better go fairly early. Half past ten?'

'Right. I'll meet you in the hall.'

Rosamund Darnley, walking out of the <u>dining room</u> after a late breakfast, was bumped into by Linda as the latter came running down the stairs.

'Oh! Sorry, Miss Darnley.'

Rosamund said, 'Lovely morning, isn't it? You can hardly believe it after yesterday.'

'I know. I'm going with Mrs Redfern to draw at Gull Cove. I said I'd meet her at half past ten. I think I'm late.'

'No, you're not – it's only twenty-five past.'

'Oh, good!'

Linda was breathing heavily.

'You haven't got a fever, have you, Linda?'

The girl's eyes were very bright, and her cheeks were red.

'Oh no, I'm fine!' she replied.

Christine Redfern came down the stairs. She was wearing enormous loose beach trousers with wide legs and a shirt with long sleeves. They were both green with a yellow design. Rosamund really wanted to tell her they were the worst colours possible for her fair skin.

She thought, 'However much of a fool Arlena is, she does know how to dress. This poor girl looks just like a lettuce that's gone off.'

Aloud she said, 'Have a nice time!'

♦ ♦ ♦

The beauty of the morning tempted Hercule Poirot to leave the hotel earlier than usual. It was ten o'clock when he went down to the swimming beach, which was empty except for one person.

Arlena Marshall.

Dressed in her white swimsuit and green sun hat, she was trying to launch a <u>float</u>. Poirot came to her rescue, helping her push off from the beach.

She thanked him, then she called to him from the sea, 'Monsieur Poirot, will you do something for me?'

'Anything.'

She smiled, 'Don't tell anyone where I am. Everyone follows me all the time. I just want to be alone for once.'

Then she began to paddle away. Poirot walked along the beach. He said to himself, 'Ah, I do not believe that.' Arlena Marshall was almost certainly meeting someone in secret, and he had a very good idea who that someone was.

But there he found he was wrong. For just as Arlena disappeared round the point of the bay, Patrick Redfern, closely followed by Kenneth Marshall, came down to the beach from the hotel.

Marshall nodded to Poirot, 'Morning, Poirot. Have you seen my wife anywhere?'

Poirot's answer was <u>diplomatic</u>. 'Is madame up so early, then?'

Marshall said, 'She's not in her room.' He looked up at the sky. 'Lovely day. I'm going to have a swim right away. Then I've got a lot of typing to do this morning.'

Patrick Redfern was looking up and down the beach. He sat down near Poirot, obviously waiting for someone to arrive.

Poirot said, 'And Madame Redfern? Was she up early, too?'

Patrick said, 'Christine? Oh, she's going off drawing.'

He spoke impatiently, his mind clearly elsewhere. As time passed, he could not hide how desperate he was for Arlena to arrive. At every <u>footstep</u> he turned his head eagerly to see who was coming down from the hotel.

Disappointment followed disappointment.

First came Mr and Mrs Gardener, complete with the usual knitting and book. Mrs Gardener settled in her chair and began to knit enthusiastically.

Marshall had just finished his swim. He came up the beach swinging his towel.

'It's pretty good in the sea this morning,' he said. 'Unfortunately, I've got a lot of work to do. I must go and get on with it.'

Patrick Redfern did not go into the water. He sat staring towards the hotel. He was beginning to look <u>sulky</u>.

Miss Brewster was energetic and cheerful when she arrived.

Poirot asked, 'Are you going to swim, mademoiselle?'

'Oh, I had my morning swim before breakfast. And somebody nearly <u>brained</u> me with a bottle while I was swimming! They must have thrown it out of one of the hotel windows.'

'Now that's a very dangerous thing to do,' said Mrs Gardener. 'I had a very dear friend who got hurt by a toothpaste tin falling on him in the street – thrown out of a thirty-fifth storey window.' She began to hunt among her balls of wool. 'Why, Odell, I don't believe I've got that purple wool. It's in the second drawer of the desk in our bedroom.'

'Yes, darling.'

Mr Gardener rose <u>obediently</u> and departed.

Emily Brewster lowered her voice. 'Where's our <u>vamp</u> this morning? She's late.'

Mrs Gardener raised her eyes to study Patrick Redfern: 'He looks like a black cloud. Oh dear, the whole thing is such a pity.'

Patrick rose and began to walk up and down the beach.

Mrs Gardener murmured, 'Just like a tiger.'

Three pairs of eyes watched him. Patrick Redfern looked more than sulky now. He was in a <u>flaming</u> temper.

Nobody said any more until Mr Gardener returned with a ball of purple wool.

'Why, Odell, what a long time you've been!' said his wife.

'Sorry darling, but you see it wasn't in your desk. I found it on your wardrobe shelf.'

'Well, isn't that strange!' Mrs Gardener said.

It was then that Patrick Redfern asked, 'Are you going for your row this morning, Miss Brewster? Do you mind if I come with you?'

Miss Brewster said cheerfully, 'I'd be delighted. Let's go.'

They went down the beach together.

♦ ◆ ♦

Patrick Redfern started rowing powerfully. The boat moved quickly through the water.

Emily Brewster approved. 'Good,' she said. 'We'll see if you can keep that up.'

Patrick laughed. His spirits had improved: 'What a marvellous day!'

They rounded the point of the bay to the west and rowed under the cliffs. Patrick looked up.

'Is there anyone on Sunny Ledge this morning? Yes, there's a sun umbrella.'

Emily said, 'It's Miss Darnley, I think.'

They rowed up the coast. On their left was the open sea. Patrick was still rowing strongly, while at the same time <u>scanning</u> the cliffs.

Emily suddenly thought, 'He's looking for the Marshall woman. That's why he wanted to come. He's wondering what she's doing.

They rowed along the shore to the south of Pixy Cove. It was a small bay, with rocks on the beach. In the morning, when the sun was off it because of the cliffs, it was not popular and there was seldom anyone there.

Now, however, there was a figure on the beach.

Patrick tried to sound casual: 'Oh look, who's that?'

Emily said, 'It looks like Mrs Marshall.'

'So it does.'

He started to row towards the shore. Emily protested, 'We don't want to land, do we?'

Patrick said quickly, 'Oh, there's plenty of time.'

His eyes looked into hers – something in them, rather like the look of a hopeful dog, <u>silenced</u> Emily.

She thought, 'The poor boy – he's <u>got it badly</u>.'

The boat approached the beach.

Arlena Marshall was lying face down on the sand, her arms out and her head covered by her hat. The float was nearby.

Something puzzled Emily. Something was wrong. It was a minute or two before she realised what it was. Arlena Marshall was lying like a sunbather. But there was no sun on Pixy Cove and there wouldn't be any for hours yet. A bad feeling came over Emily Brewster.

The boat landed. Patrick called, 'Hello, Arlena.'

The figure did not move or answer.

Patrick Redfern's face changed. He jumped out of the boat and Emily followed.

Patrick got there first but Emily was close behind him. She saw, as you see in a dream, the suntan, the white swimsuit, the red curl of hair escaping from under the green hat; she saw something else too – the unnatural <u>angle</u> of the arms. This body had not lain down but had been thrown down.

She heard Patrick's voice – a frightened whisper. She stood back as he bent down – touched the hand – the arm…

He said in an awful whisper, 'She's dead!'

And then, as he lifted the hat a little and saw her neck: 'No! She's been <u>strangled</u>… *murdered!*'

◆ ◆ ◆

It was one of those moments when time stands still.

With an odd feeling of <u>unreality</u>, Emily Brewster heard herself saying, 'We mustn't touch anything – not until the police come.'

Redfern's answer came <u>mechanically</u>. 'No. No – of course not.' And then in a deep, <u>agonized</u> whisper. 'Who? *Who?* Who could have done this to Arlena?'

Emily shook her head, not knowing what to answer. She shivered.

Then she heard her voice saying, 'We must get the police—' She hesitated, then said: 'One of us should stay with... the body.'

Patrick said, 'I'll stay.'

Emily Brewster sighed with relief, grateful not to have to remain on that beach alone with a possible murderer close by.

'I'll be as quick as I can. I'll go in the boat. I can't face that ladder,' she said.

Patrick murmured mechanically, 'Yes – yes, whatever you think best.'

As Emily rowed quickly away from the shore, she saw Patrick drop down beside the dead woman and put his head in his hands. He looked like a dog watching its dead master.

CHAPTER 5

Inspector[9] Colgate stood by the cliff waiting for the doctor to finish examining Arlena's body. Emily Brewster and Patrick Redfern stood to one side.

Dr Neasdon rose from his knees.

'Strangled – by a powerful pair of hands. She doesn't seem to have struggled. She must have been taken by surprise.'

Inspector Colgate asked, 'What about the time of death?'

Neasdon said, 'It's quarter to one now. What time was it when you found her?'

Patrick said, 'Some time before twelve. I don't know.'

Emily said with certainty, 'It was quarter to twelve.'

'Ah, and you came here in the boat,' continued the Inspector. 'What time was it when you first saw her lying here?'

Emily Brewster considered: 'I would say we came round the coast about five minutes earlier.'

Neasdon said, 'Let's say at twenty minutes to twelve, then. She can't have been killed long before that. Let's say it happened between then and eleven – at quarter to eleven at the earliest.'

The Inspector shut his notebook.

'Thanks,' he said. 'That should help us considerably. It puts the time of the murder within very narrow limits.'

'I don't believe it!' said Colonel[3] Weston, the Chief Constable[9]. 'This is a surprise finding you here!'

Hercule Poirot replied, 'Ah, yes, many years have passed since that interesting case at St Loo.'

'I haven't forgotten it, though,' said Weston. 'It was the biggest surprise of my life. I'd never seen anything like it. Fantastic! And here you are in the middle of another murder. Any ideas about this one?'

'Nothing definite,' Poirot said. 'But it is interesting.'

'Are you going to give us a hand?'

'Would you permit me to?'

'My dear man, I'd be delighted to have you. First, we've got to find out who last saw the dead woman alive.'

'*Mon ami* – my friend,' said Poirot, 'I suspect I am the man you want. I assisted her to launch her float from near the hotel. I would say she left the beach at around quarter past ten.'

Weston considered this.

'It would take her perhaps half an hour to paddle round to the Cove,' he said. 'If she arrived there at quarter to eleven, that fits well enough. The doctor suggests that the earliest time she died is quarter to eleven.'

Poirot nodded.

'There is one other point I must mention,' he said. 'As she left, Mrs Marshall asked me not to say I had seen her.'

Weston stared at him: 'Hmm, that's rather interesting, isn't it?'

'Yes. I thought so.'

Weston played with his moustache.

'Look here, Poirot. Was it true? Was Mrs Marshall having a relationship with Patrick Redfern?'

'Yes, I am sure she was.'

'And her husband? Did he know about it? What did he feel?'

Poirot said slowly, 'It is not easy to know what Captain Marshall feels or thinks. He is not a man who shows his emotions.'

♦ ◆ ♦

Mrs Castle, the owner of the Jolly Roger Hotel, was a woman of about forty with blonde hair and a polite manner.

She was saying, 'I can't believe that such a thing has happened in my hotel! The guests who come here are such nice people. Not like the big hotels in St Loo. And of course, no one but hotel guests are allowed on the island.'

'How do you keep people off the island?' Inspector Colgate asked.

'There are notices. And then, of course, at <u>high tide</u>, we are cut off.'

'Yes, but at <u>low tide</u>?'

Mrs Castle explained that at the island end of the causeway[2] there was a gate. This said 'Jolly Roger Hotel. Private. No entry except to the hotel.' The rocks rose <u>sheer</u> out of the sea on either side and could not be climbed.

Anyone could take a boat, of course, and row round to one of the coves. You can't stop people being on the beaches.

But this, she said, very seldom happened. Although people could hire boats at Leathercombe Bay harbour, it was a long way to the island, and there was a strong <u>current</u>. She added that George and William were always <u>on the lookout</u> at the swimming beach, which was the nearest to the mainland.

'Who are George and William?'

'George looks after the swimming beach. William is the gardener.'

Colonel Weston said, 'Well, that seems clear enough. Anyone who comes from outside, risks being noticed. We'll have a word with George and William. Now then, Mrs Castle, have you got a list of the guests staying here?'

'Yes, sir.'

Weston looked carefully at the hotel register. He looked over at Poirot:

'This is where you'll be able to help us, I think, Poirot. Now, Mrs Castle, what about staff?'

Mrs Castle produced a second list.

'There are four <u>chambermaids</u>, the head waiter, three other waiters and Henry in the bar. Then there's the cook and two others who work with her.'

'Tell me about the waiters.'

'Well, sir, Albert, the head waiter, came to me from the Vincent Hotel in Plymouth. He was there for many years. The waiters under him have all been here for three years. Very nice boys and most respectable.'

Weston nodded, then said to Inspector Colgate, 'You'll check up on them, of course. Thank you, Mrs Castle. We'll speak with Captain Marshall first.'

♦ ◆ ♦

Kenneth Marshall sat quietly answering the questions he was asked. His face looked tense but he was calm. Seen here, with the sunlight falling on him from the window, you realized that he was a handsome man. He had straight features, nice blue eyes and a firm mouth. His voice was low and pleasant.

Colonel Weston was saying, 'Captain Marshall, I understand what a shock this must be for you. But I am anxious to get the fullest information as soon as possible.'

Marshall nodded. 'I understand. Carry on.'

'Mrs Marshall was your second wife? An actress?'

'Yes. We've been married for four years. Her acting name was Arlena Stuart.'

'Did she give up acting when you got married?' asked Weston.

'No,' replied Marshall. 'She only stopped about a year and a half ago.'

'Was there any special reason why she stopped then?'

Kenneth Marshall appeared to consider this.

'No,' he replied. 'She simply said that she was tired of it all.'

'So you hadn't asked her to give up acting? It wasn't causing arguments between you?'

'Certainly not. My wife was free to do whatever she wanted.'

Weston paused for a moment. Then he said, 'Captain Marshall, have you any idea who could have killed your wife?'

'None whatsoever.'

'Did she have any enemies?'

'Possibly. My wife was an actress. She was also a very attractive woman. Many people were jealous of her. But not enough to murder her.'

Hercule Poirot spoke for the first time: 'Do you mean, monsieur, that her enemies were women?'

Kenneth Marshall looked across at him: 'Yes.'

The Chief Constable said, 'Did she already know anyone staying at this hotel?'

'I believe she had met Mr Redfern before – at a party.'

Weston said, 'When was the last time you saw your wife?'

'I went to her room on my way down to breakfast, about nine o'clock.'

'Excuse me, so you had separate rooms?'

'Yes.'

'What was she doing when you visited her?'

'Opening her letters.'

'Did she say anything?'

'Just good morning, that it was a nice day – that sort of thing.'

'What was her manner like? Was it unusual at all?'

Marshall thought for a moment. 'No, she was perfectly normal.'

Poirot said, 'Did she mention the contents of her letters?'

A faint smile appeared on Marshall's lips: 'She said they were all bills.'

Poirot asked, 'Did your wife have breakfast in her room?'

'Yes. Always.'

Poirot said, 'What time did she usually come downstairs?'

'Usually around eleven.'

Poirot went on, 'But this morning she came down at ten. Why do you think that was, Captain Marshall?'

Marshall said without emotion, 'I have no idea. I went to see her again after breakfast and her room was empty. I was a bit surprised.'

'And then you came down to the beach and asked me if I had seen her?'

'Yes... And you said you hadn't.'

Poirot maintained his innocent expression. Gently, he stroked his large and <u>flamboyant</u> moustache.

Weston said, 'Just now, Captain Marshall, you mentioned that your wife had previously met Mr Patrick Redfern. How well did your wife actually know Mr Redfern?'

Marshall looked back at the Chief Constable.

'Do you mind if I smoke?' He felt through his pockets. 'Oh, where on earth is my pipe?'

Poirot offered him a cigarette.

Lighting it, Marshall said, 'You were asking about Redfern.'

'I understand,' the Chief Constable said, 'that their friendship had become something closer.'

Marshall said sharply, 'You understand that, do you? Who told you that?'

'It's common gossip in the hotel, Captain.'

For a moment there was a cold anger in Marshall's eyes: 'Hotel gossip is usually lies!'

'Possibly. But I have heard that Mr Redfern and your wife were constantly in each other's company.'

'I really didn't notice.'

'You didn't object to your wife's friendship with Mr Redfern?'

'I wasn't in the habit of <u>interfering</u> in my wife's friendships.'

'You didn't say anything? Even though it was becoming a scandal, and it was damaging Mr and Mrs Redfern's marriage?'

Kenneth Marshall said, 'I <u>mind my own business</u> and I expect other people to mind theirs. I don't listen to gossip.'

'You don't deny that Mr Redfern admired your wife?'

'Most men did. She was a beautiful woman.'

'But you believed that there was nothing serious in the affair?'

'I honestly never thought about it.'

'What would you say if I said we have a witness who knows that they were more than just friends?'

Marshall's blue eyes looked briefly at Poirot.

He said, 'If you want to listen to these tales, listen to them. My wife's dead and can't defend herself.'

'You mean that you, personally, don't believe them?'

For the first time, a faint line of sweat could be seen on Marshall's forehead.

'No,' he said, 'and I don't intend to either. Anything else?'

'Yes, Captain Marshall, please tell us everything you did this morning.'

'I had breakfast downstairs at about nine. As I told you, I went up to my wife's room, then down to the beach and asked

Monsieur Poirot if he had seen her. Then I had a quick swim and went up to the hotel again. The clock downstairs said it was twenty to eleven. I went up to my room, but the chambermaid hadn't finished cleaning it. I asked her to finish as quickly as she could because I had some letters to type, which I wanted to send in the next post.

I went downstairs, then returned to my room at ten minutes to eleven. I typed until ten to twelve, then changed into my tennis clothes as I was playing tennis at twelve. Miss Darnley and Mr Gardener were at the tennis court. Mrs Redfern arrived a few minutes later. We played for an hour and afterwards I— I got the news about my wife...'

'Thank you, Captain Marshall. Is there anyone who can corroborate these facts?'

Kenneth Marshall said with a faint smile, 'Do you think that I killed my wife?'

Weston said smoothly, 'Everyone on the island will be asked the same question, Captain Marshall.'

'Well, let me see now. The chambermaid who cleaned my room. Then there are the letters themselves. I haven't posted them yet. You'll see that it would have taken me at least an hour to type them out.'

He took three letters from his pocket. 'Their contents are private – I presume I can count on the discretion of the police. They contain financial statements.'

Weston took the letters from Marshall: 'Thank you. One more thing – do you know if your wife had made a will?'

'Her lawyers are Barkett & Applegood, Bedford Square. But I'm fairly certain she never made a will – she said it would give her the shivers.'

'If she never made a will, then you, as her husband, will get all her property.'

'I suppose that's true.'

'Did she have any relatives?'

'If she had, she never mentioned them. Her parents died when she was a child and she didn't have any brothers or sisters.'

'Anyway, I suppose, she didn't have very much money to leave?'

Kenneth Marshall said coldly, 'On the contrary. Only two years ago, Sir Robert Erskine, who was an old friend of hers, died and left her about fifty thousand pounds.'

Inspector Colgate looked up quickly, and said, 'Then actually, Captain Marshall, your wife was a rich woman?'

Kenneth Marshall said, 'Yes, I suppose she was. Is there anything else?'

Weston shook his head:

'Once more, Captain Marshall, let me offer you all my sympathy concerning your loss.'

Marshall went out.

Chapter 6

Colonel Weston, Inspector Colgate and Hercule Poirot looked at each other.

Weston said, 'What do you think of Marshall, Colgate?'

The Inspector shook his head: 'It's difficult to tell. He's not the kind that shows anything.'

Poirot raised his hands: 'He is a closed box. He has heard nothing, seen nothing, knows nothing!'

'We've got a choice of motives,' said Colgate. 'Someone who was jealous of Mrs Marshall, or someone who wanted her money. Her husband's the obvious suspect. If he knew his wife was having a relationship with—'

Poirot interrupted: '*Écoute, mon ami* – listen, my friend. Last night I saw those two together – Mrs Marshall and Patrick Redfern. And a moment later, I met Captain Marshall. His face told me that he knew about them for sure. But even then, what does that tell us? What did Kenneth Marshall feel about his wife?'

'And his alibi is his typewriter,' said Weston with a short bark of a laugh. 'What about that, Colgate?'

Inspector Colgate did not look impressed: 'Well, sir, if the chambermaid was nearby and heard the typewriter, then it looks to me like we'll have to look elsewhere for the murderer.'

'Hmmm,' said Weston, 'Where would you look?'

For a minute or two the three men thought about this question. Then Colgate said, 'Motive is the most important thing. And all the motives point to Captain Marshall. If the motive is money, the only person to gain by her death was the lady's husband. If the motive is jealousy, and her husband says she didn't have any real enemies – though I don't believe that – then isn't he the person with the most reason to be jealous? What do you say, Monsieur Poirot?'

Poirot responded, 'Arlena Marshall's enemies would, as I said, be women, Inspector. And it does not seem possible that this crime was committed by a woman. What does the medical evidence say?'

Weston grunted: 'Dr Neasdon's confident that she was strangled by a man.'

Poirot nodded: 'Exactly. It is a man we have to look for. And yet there is only one other person who has a strong and obvious motive.'

'Redfern's wife,' said Weston.

'Yes. Mrs Redfern had a good reason to kill Arlena Stuart,' said Poirot. 'But to strangle her, no. She is not capable of having committed this crime – her hands are too small.'

Weston nodded: 'Yes, a man did this.'

Poirot said, 'And this morning, when Arlena Marshall asked me not to tell anyone I had seen her, I at once thought she was going to meet Patrick Redfern and did not want her husband to know.'

He paused.

'But I was wrong – because, although her husband appeared almost immediately on the beach, Patrick Redfern also arrived – and was obviously looking for her! And therefore, my friends, I am asking myself, *who was it that Arlena Marshall went to meet?*'

Weston sighed and shook his head: 'We can discuss theories later. We've got to get through these interviews now. To work out where everyone was. We'd better see the Marshall girl now.'

Linda Marshall was breathing quickly when she entered the room, and she seemed nervous.

'Poor kid,' thought Weston. 'This must have been a bad shock for her.'

He invited her to sit down and said in a <u>reassuring</u> voice, 'We're sorry to put you through this, Miss— Linda, isn't it?'

'Yes, Linda.'

The girl had a schoolgirl's voice.

Weston thought, 'A kid shouldn't be involved in this sort of thing.'

He said, 'We just want you to tell us anything you know that might be useful, that's all.'

Linda said, 'You mean about Arlena?'

'Yes. Did you see her this morning?'

The girl shook her head: 'No. Arlena always comes down late. She has breakfast in her room.'

Poirot said, 'And you, mademoiselle?'

'Oh, I got up. I had a swim and then breakfast, and then I went with Mrs Redfern to Gull Cove.'

Weston said, 'What time did you and Mrs Redfern leave the hotel?'

'She said she'd be waiting for me in the hall at half past ten. I was afraid I was going to be late, but it was all right. We left at about three minutes before half past ten.'

Poirot said, 'And what did you do at Gull Cove?'

'Oh, I sunbathed, and Mrs Redfern painted. Then, later, I went into the sea and Christine went back to the hotel to get changed for tennis.'

Weston said, keeping his voice casual, 'Do you remember what time that was?'

'Yes, quarter to twelve. I looked at my watch.'

Weston said, 'Do you mind if I see your watch?'

Linda held out her wrist. He compared the watch with his own and with the hotel clock on the wall.

He said, smiling, 'It's correct to a second. And you got back to the hotel – when?'

'Just about one o'clock. And— and then— I heard about Arlena...'

Weston said, 'Did you, er... get on with your stepmother all right?'

She looked at him for a minute without replying. Then she said, 'Oh, yes. Arlena was kind to me.'

Weston went on, 'Families can have all sorts of problems – quarrels, arguments, you know. Was there anything like that?'

Linda said, 'Do you mean, did Father and Arlena quarrel?'

'Well, yes.'

Linda said, 'Oh no. Father doesn't quarrel with people. He's not like that.'

Weston said, 'Thank you. Now, Miss Linda, I want you to think very carefully. Do you have any idea at all who might have killed your stepmother?'

Linda gave the question serious consideration. She said at last, 'No, I don't know who could have wanted to kill Arlena.' Then she added, 'Except, of course, Mrs Redfern.'

'You think Mrs Redfern wanted to kill her? Why?'

'Well, because her husband was in love with Arlena,' replied Linda. 'But I don't think she would really want to *kill* her. I mean, she'd just wish she was dead – and that isn't the same thing, is it?'

Poirot said gently, 'No, it is not the same at all.'

Linda nodded. A look of distress passed across her face. She said, 'And anyway, Mrs Redfern could never kill anybody like that. She isn't violent, if you know what I mean.'

Weston and Poirot nodded. The latter said, 'I know exactly what you mean, my child – Mrs Redfern is not someone who, as your saying goes, "<u>sees red</u>". She would not' – he leaned back, choosing his words carefully – 'do something in one emotional moment – seeing a hated face, a hated neck, feeling her hands make fists, wishing to feel them press into flesh—'

He stopped.

Linda moved <u>unsteadily</u> back from the table. She said in a trembling voice, 'Can I go now? Is that all?'

Weston said, 'Yes, yes, that's all. Thank you, Miss Linda.'

He got up to open the door for her, then came back to the table. 'Phew,' he said. 'Not a nice job, questioning that child. Inviting a daughter to put a rope round her father's neck[10]. All the same, it had to be done.'

He gave an embarrassed cough: 'By the way, Poirot, you went a bit far there. All that "hands pressing into flesh" business! Not the sort of idea to put into a kid's head.'

Poirot looked at him thoughtfully. He said, 'So you think I put ideas into her head?'

'Well, didn't you?'

Poirot shook his head.

Weston moved on.

'Well, we got an alibi for Christine Redfern anyway – she was at Gull Cove with Linda at the time of the murder. So the jealous wife can't be a suspect. I suppose we'd better see the Redferns next.'

◆ ◆ ◆

Patrick Redfern came in first. He looked pale and ill and very young, but his manner was now <u>composed</u>.

Colonel Weston asked, 'Mr Redfern, how long had you known Mrs Marshall?'

Patrick Redfern hesitated, then said, 'Three months.'

Weston went on: 'Captain Marshall has told us that you met her at a party. Is that right?'

'Yes.' Again, Patrick hesitated. Then he said, 'As a matter of fact, I saw quite a lot of her after that.'

'Without Captain Marshall's knowledge?'

Redfern's face went red:

'I don't know whether he knew or not.'

Poirot spoke, 'And was it also without your wife's knowledge, Mr Redfern?'

'I mentioned I had met the famous Arlena Stuart.'

Poirot persisted, 'But she did not know how often?'

'Well, perhaps not.'

Weston said, 'Did you and Mrs Marshall arrange to meet down here?'

Redfern said, 'I suppose it's bound to come out now. I was crazy about the woman – mad – totally in love with her. She wanted me to come down here. I agreed. I— Well, I would have agreed to do anything she asked. She had that effect on people.'

Poirot murmured, 'You paint a very clear picture of her.'

Patrick Redfern said bitterly, 'As I say, I was in love with her. Whether she cared for me or not, I don't know. I think she was one of those women who loses interest in a man once she's got him. Well, she definitely knew she'd got me. This morning, when I found her there on the beach, dead, it was as though...' He paused. 'As though something had hit me straight between the eyes.'

Poirot leaned forward. 'And now?'

Patrick Redfern met his eyes: 'I know I haven't thought much about my wife up to now. But, though you may find this difficult to believe, the truth is I care for her very deeply. The thing with Arlena was madness – the kind of stupid, foolish thing men do – but Christine is different. She's real. I've treated her badly, but I've known all along, deep down, that she was the person who was really important to me.' He paused, sighed, then said rather pathetically, 'I wish I could make you believe that.'

Poirot leant forward: 'But I do believe it.'

Weston cleared his throat: 'Mr Redfern, what you don't seem to realize is that that relationship might be a motive for the crime.'

'Motive?' Patrick asked. 'What? You mean Marshall found out and— and killed her?' Redfern shook his head: 'No, never. He's such a quiet man.'

'Monsieur Redfern, was there, at any time, the question of a divorce?' Poirot asked.

Patrick Redfern shook his head.

'Oh no. There was Christine, you see. And Arlena was perfectly satisfied married to Marshall. He's rich. She never thought of me as a possible husband. No, I was just one of a long line of poor fools. I knew that all along, and yet it didn't alter my feelings towards her…'

He sat there thinking.

Weston brought him back to the moment: 'Now, Mr Redfern, did you have a meeting planned with Mrs Marshall this morning?'

Patrick Redfern looked puzzled.

'Not a particular meeting, no. We usually met every morning on the beach.'

'Were you surprised not to find Mrs Marshall there this morning?'

'Yes, I was. Very surprised.'

'Do you know any reason why Mrs Marshall may have gone to Pixy Cove?'

Redfern shook his head: 'I really have no idea!'

Weston said, 'Please think very carefully. Is there anyone who could have had a <u>grudge</u> against Mrs Marshall? Someone, for instance, whom she may have liked before she liked you?'

Redfern thought for some minutes. Then he shook his head: 'Honestly, I can't think of anyone.'

Weston drummed with his fingers on the table. He said at last, 'Well, we seem to have two people on this island who had a motive for killing her. Her husband and your wife.'

Redfern stared at him. He looked confused: 'My wife? Christine? Do you mean that Christine had something to do with this?' He got up, <u>stammering</u> as he tried to get the words out too quickly: 'You're mad – mad! Christine? It's impossible. It's ridiculous!'

Weston said, 'Mr Redfern, jealousy is a powerful motive. Women who are jealous lose control of themselves completely.'

Redfern said in a very serious voice, 'Not Christine. She's not like that. She was unhappy, yes. But— oh, she's not violent. Besides, it would be absurd. Arlena was twice as strong as Christine. And then Christine could never have got down that ladder to the beach – she doesn't like heights. It's ridiculous!'

♦ ◆ ♦

When Redfern had left the room, the Chief Constable said with a smile, 'I didn't think it was necessary to tell the man his wife had got an alibi. I wanted to hear what he'd have to say to the idea. It upset him, didn't it?'

Poirot said, 'His arguments were as strong as any alibi.'

'Yes. She couldn't have done it – she isn't strong enough. Marshall could have done it – but apparently, he didn't. We must—'

He broke off as Christine Redfern entered the room. She was, as always, calm.

She was wearing a white tennis dress and a pale blue jumper. It suited her fair prettiness. Yet, Poirot thought it was neither a silly face nor a weak one. It had plenty of determination and courage.

Colonel Weston said, 'Take a seat, Mrs Redfern. We're asking everybody for an account of their morning.'

Christine Redfern said in her quiet voice, 'Oh yes, I understand. Let me see. On my way down to breakfast I went into Linda Marshall's room and arranged with her to go to Gull Cove.'

'Excuse me, madame,' Poirot said. 'What time did you go to Miss Marshall's room?'

'Let me see… half past eight – no, a little later.'

'And was Miss Marshall up then?'

'Oh yes, she'd already been out.'

'Out?' Weston asked.

'Yes, she said she'd been swimming.'

Weston said, 'And after breakfast?'

'I collected my painting box and we left the hotel. I think it was just half past ten. At Gull Cove, I drew and painted, and Linda sunbathed.'

'What time did you leave the cove?'

'At quarter to twelve. I was playing tennis at twelve.'

'You had your watch with you?'

'No, as a matter of fact I didn't. I asked Linda the time.'

'I see. And then?'

'I packed up my things and went back to the hotel.'

Poirot said, 'And Mademoiselle Linda?'

'Linda? Oh, Linda went into the sea. She was splashing in the waves as I went up the cliff path.'

'Go on, Mrs Redfern,' Weston said.

'I changed and went to the tennis court where I met the others. Then the news came about Mrs Marshall. It was horrible.'

Poirot leant forward.

'Madame, as a woman of intelligence and good sense, were you really surprised at the manner of Mrs Marshall's death?'

Christine said, 'No, I wasn't. Shocked, yes. But she was the kind of woman—'

She hesitated, and Poirot finished the sentence for her.

'To whom such a thing might happen. Yes, madame, that is the truest and most significant thing that has been said in this room this morning. What did you really think of Mrs Marshall?'

Christine Redfern said calmly, 'Is it really worthwhile talking about all that now?'

'I think it might be, yes.'

'Well, what shall I say?' Her fair skin was suddenly full of colour. Her careful calm was lost: 'She was useless! She did nothing to justify her existence. She had no mind – no brains. She thought of nothing but men and clothes and being admired. Useless! She lived for that kind of life. And so, no, I wasn't surprised by her death. She was the sort of woman who would be mixed up with everything bad – blackmail, jealousy, violence… She— she appealed to the worst in people.'

She stopped, breathing quickly. Her rather short top lip lifted itself in <u>disgust</u>.

It occurred to Colonel Weston that you could not have found a more complete contrast to Arlena Stuart than Christine Redfern. And then a single word caught his attention.

He leaned forward: 'Mrs Redfern, why did you mention blackmail?'

Christine stared at him:

'I suppose… because she was being blackmailed.'

CHAPTER 7

Christine Redfern said awkwardly, 'I— I heard something...'

Weston said, 'Will you explain, please, Mrs Redfern?'

Christine's face turned red. She said, 'It was three nights ago. We were playing bridge[11]. It was very warm in the card room, so I went out for a breath of fresh air. I went down towards the beach and I suddenly heard voices. One – it was Arlena Marshall's – said, "It's no good asking me. I can't get any more money now. My husband will suspect something." And then a man's voice said, "I'm not taking any excuses. You've got to <u>cough up</u>." And then Arlena said, "You blackmailing <u>brute</u>!" And the man said, "Brute or not, you'll pay, my lady."'

Weston said, 'Do you know who the man was?'

Christine Redfern shook her head. 'His voice was gruff and he was keeping it low,' she replied. 'I barely heard what he said. It— oh, it could have been anybody.'

♦ ♦ ♦

When the door had closed behind Christine Redfern, Inspector Colgate said, 'Now we're getting somewhere! Somebody in this hotel was blackmailing the lady.'

Poirot said, 'But it is not the <u>blackmailer</u> who lies dead. It is the victim. That is odd, is it not?'

'That's true, I agree,' said the Inspector. 'But it gives us a reason for Mrs Marshall's behaviour this morning. She'd got a secret meeting with this blackmailer.'

'It certainly explains why she went off on her own,' agreed Poirot.

Colgate went on: 'And the place chosen, Pixy Cove – no one goes there in the morning because it doesn't have the sun until later in the day.'

Poirot said, 'It is, as you say, ideal for a meeting. It is empty. It is only accessible from the land side by a steep steel ladder. Moreover, most of the beach is invisible from above. And it has another advantage – Mr Redfern told me there is a hidden cave. Anyone could wait there without being seen.'

Weston said, 'Of course, Pixy's Cave.'

Colgate said, 'We'd better have a look inside it.'

'Yes, you're right,' Weston agreed. 'But who was it she went there to meet? Presumably someone staying in this hotel.'

He drew the hotel register towards him.

'We've got the following men: the American – Gardener, Major Barry, Horace Blatt, and Stephen Lane.'

'Major Barry went out at ten o'clock this morning. He returned at half past one,' Colgate said. 'Mr Lane had breakfast at eight. He said he was going for a <u>hike</u>. Mr Blatt went off for a sail at half past nine, the same as he does most days. Neither of them are back yet.'

'A sail, eh?' Weston's voice was thoughtful.

'Well, we'll interview them all,' Weston said. 'We might learn something about the blackmailing.'

Mr and Mrs Gardener came in together.

'Of course, I said, we're anxious to help the British police in any way we can,' Mrs Gardener announced as soon as they were in the room. 'So go right ahead and ask me anything at all—'

Colonel Weston opened his mouth at this invitation but had to wait while Mrs Gardener went on, 'That's what I said, Odell, isn't it?'

'Yes, darling,' said Mr Gardener.

Weston spoke quickly.

'I understand, Mrs Gardener, that you and your husband were on the beach all morning?'

'Yes, certainly we were,' said Mrs Gardener. 'And that young man, Mr Redfern – so impatient he was, so cross about everything. And I said to myself, *why*, when he has that nice pretty little wife, must he go running after that dreadful woman? I always felt that about her, didn't I, Odell?'

'Yes, darling.'

'How that nice Captain Marshall came to marry such a woman I cannot imagine – and with that nice young daughter. It's so important for girls to have the right influence. Mrs Marshall was not at all the right person – the wrong background entirely – and I would say the wrong nature too. Now if Captain Marshall had had any sense, he'd have married Miss Darnley, who's a very charming and distinguished woman. You only have to look at Rosamund Darnley to see she's just full of brains. I admire that woman more than I can say. And I said to Mr Gardener the other day that anyone could see she was crazy about Captain Marshall, didn't I, Odell?'

'Yes, darling.'

'I'm not a <u>narrow-minded</u> woman, Colonel Weston – in fact, a lot of my best friends are actresses – but I've said to Mr Gardener all along that there was something evil about that woman. And you see, I've been proved right.'

She paused.

Hercule Poirot's lips bent into a little smile.

Weston said rather desperately, 'Well, thank you, Mrs Gardener. I suppose there's nothing that either of you has noticed that might be relevant to the case?'

Poirot spoke. 'Perhaps, Mr Gardener, when you went back to the hotel to get the wool for Mrs Gardener?' Then he continued, 'Maybe you saw something, or perhaps you saw someone, and you wished them *une bonne journée* – a good day...?'

'No, I didn't see a soul. And I don't think I can add anything relevant,' Mr Gardener said in a slow American accent. 'Mrs Marshall hung around with young Redfern most of the time – but everybody can tell you that.'

◆ ◆ ◆

Major Barry was trying to look <u>horrified</u> but could not quite manage it.

He said, 'I'm glad to help. Of course I don't know anything.'

Colonel Weston asked, 'You didn't see Mrs Marshall at all this morning?'

'I didn't see anybody this morning. I went over to St Loo. Just my luck – this is the sort of place here where nothing happens for months, and when it does, you miss it!'

Weston prompted him, 'So you went to St Loo, you say?'

'Yes, I wanted to make some telephone calls. Private telephone calls.' The Major winked cheerfully. 'A bit of business with a friend of mine. I couldn't get through to him, unfortunately. I only got back half an hour ago.'

Weston said, 'Did you speak to anyone in St Loo?'

Barry laughed, 'So you want me to prove an alibi, do you? I saw about fifty thousand people in St Loo – but that doesn't mean they'll remember seeing me.'

Inspector Colgate saw the Major out. Coming back, he said, 'It's going to be difficult to check up on anything in St Loo. It's the middle of the holiday season.'

The Chief Constable said, 'It's possible he parked somewhere, walked back here and went to the cove. But it would have been risky – he couldn't count on no one seeing him.'

Colgate nodded: 'He could have gone to the cove by boat.'

Weston agreed, 'That's more likely. If he'd had a boat in one of the coves nearby, he could have left the car, rowed to Pixy Cove and rowed back. Well, I'll leave that to you, Colgate. We'd better see Miss Brewster now.'

◆ ◆ ◆

'It's a distressing business,' Emily Brewster said after she had told her story. 'However, I expect you'll soon solve it. It shouldn't be difficult.'

'Now what do you mean by that, Miss Brewster?' Colonel Weston asked.

'I meant that the woman was a bad person. You've only got to hunt around a bit in her past to find things.'

Poirot said gently, 'You did not like her?'

'I know too much about her. My first cousin is married to one of the Erskines. You've probably heard, that woman got old Sir Robert to leave most of his fortune to her instead of to his own family.'

Weston said, 'And the family were angry about that?'

'Naturally. His connection with her was a scandal anyway, and then to leave her fifty thousand pounds shows the kind of woman she was. I'm sure I sound hard, but in my opinion the Arlena Stuarts of this world deserve very little sympathy. I know something else too – there was a young man who fell completely in love with her. Because of her he did something illegal – to get money to spend on her – and only just managed to escape prison. That woman <u>contaminated</u> everyone she met. No, I'm afraid I can't have any regret about her death.'

'And you think the murderer was someone from her past?'

'Yes, I do.'

Weston said, 'You may be right, Miss Brewster.'

'I'm sure I'm right,' Miss Brewster said, and went out.

◆ ◆ ◆

As always, Hercule Poirot felt a sense of pleasure at the sight of Rosamund Darnley. She sat down opposite Colonel Weston and turned a serious face to him.

'I don't think I can tell you anything that will help.'

'Knowing what you did this morning will help us, Miss Darnley.'

'Well, I had breakfast at about half past nine. Then I went up to my room and collected some books and my sun umbrella and went out to Sunny Ledge. That must have been at about twenty-five past ten. I came back about ten minutes to twelve and played tennis until lunchtime.'

'Did you see Mrs Marshall this morning?'

'No.'

'While you were at Sunny Ledge, did you notice anyone come by on a float or in a boat?'

'No, I was reading. Of course, I looked up from time to time, but the sea was empty each time.'

'So you didn't notice Mr Redfern and Miss Brewster when they rowed round to Pixy Cove?'

'No.'

'Did you ever hear that Mrs Marshall was being blackmailed, Miss Darnley?'

A look of astonishment came over Rosamund Darnley's face.

'Blackmailed? Arlena? What could anyone blackmail Arlena about?'

'Things that Mrs Marshall might be anxious should not come to her husband's ears?'

'Arlena never pretended to be respectable. That was no secret.'

'You think, then, that her husband was aware of her – friendships with other people?'

There was a pause.

At last, in a slow voice, Rosamund said, 'I don't know what to think. I've always assumed he accepted his wife for what she was – that he knew the truth about her. But that may not be true. Kenneth Marshall is not really as sophisticated as he seems. I suppose he *may* have believed in her.'

CHAPTER 8

The bedroom that had been Arlena Marshall's had two big windows and a balcony that overlooked the swimming beach and the sea beyond. Sunshine poured into the room, flashing over the bottles and jars on Arlena's <u>dressing table</u>. Every kind of beauty product was there.

Inspector Colgate, who was opening drawers, found a packet of letters. He and Colonel Weston looked through them together.

Hercule Poirot was looking at the many dresses and suits that hung in the wardrobe.

'Three of these letters are from young Redfern,' Weston said. 'Silly young fool. There's one other letter here.'

He held it out and Poirot took it.

Darling Arlena, I feel so depressed. To be going out to China and perhaps not seeing you again for years. I didn't know any man could go on feeling about a woman like I feel about you. Thanks for the cheque. They won't <u>prosecute</u> now. It was a close thing, though, and all because I wanted to make big money for you. Can you forgive me? I wanted to put diamonds in your ears – your lovely, lovely ears – and great milk-white jewels round your throat. Don't forget me – but you won't, I know. You're mine – always.

Goodbye – goodbye – goodbye.
J.N.

Colgate said, 'It might be worth finding out if J.N. really did go to China. It sounds to me as though this is the boy Miss Brewster mentioned.'

Poirot nodded: 'Yes, I think this letter is very important.'

They went into Kenneth Marshall's room.

It was next door to his wife's and also had two windows, but it was much smaller. A mirror hung on the wall between the windows. In the corner on the right was the dressing table. In the corner by the left-hand window was a writing table. A typewriter stood on it with a pile of papers beside it.

Colgate went through the papers quickly: 'Everything seems straightforward enough.' He sat down. 'I'll have a thorough look at them all and check how long it would have taken Captain Marshall to type his three letters.'

Weston said, 'We'll leave you to it and look at the rest of the rooms.'

They went into Linda Marshall's room next. It faced east, looking out over the rocks down to the sea below.

Weston looked round. 'I don't suppose there's anything to see here,' he said.

He went out again.

Poirot stayed. Something had been burnt in the fire <u>grate</u> recently. There was some candle <u>wax</u>; some pieces of green cardboard; a pin, and something burnt – it might have been hair.

Poirot stared.

'Well, what am I to make of this collection?' he said to himself. '*C'est fantastique!* It is bizarre!'

And then he picked up the pin and his eyes grew sharp and green.

'*Non!* No! It cannot be! Is it possible?'

Poirot slowly looked round the room and this time there was an entirely new expression on his face. It was very serious and almost severe.

To the left of the grate, there were some shelves with a row of books. Poirot looked thoughtfully along the titles. His eye caught sight of a book that had been pushed behind the other books.

He took it out and opened it. He nodded his head. 'So I was right… Yes. But about the other thing – is that possible too? No, it is not possible, unless…'

He stayed there, stroking his moustache while his mind raced quickly over the problem.

He said again, softly, '*Unless*—'

Colonel Weston looked in at the door: 'Hello, Poirot, are you still here?'

'I am coming!' cried Poirot. He hurried out into the corridor. The room next to Linda's was the Redferns' – but it did not interest him.

Next was Rosamund Darnley's room, where he lingered for a moment. Gently, there came to his nose the expensive perfume that Rosamund Darnley used.

Next to Rosamund Darnley's room, at the northern end of the corridor, was another door. From this, outside stairs led down to the rocks below.

Weston said, 'That's the way people go down to swim before breakfast.'

Poirot looked interested. He stepped outside and looked down. Below, a path led to steps which continued down across the rocks to the sea. There was also a path that led round the hotel to the left.

'Someone could go down these stairs,' he remarked, 'then go to the left and join the main path up from the causeway.'

Weston nodded: 'Anyone could go right across the island without going through the hotel. But they might still be seen from a window.'

'You mean Captain Marshall?' asked Poirot.

'Yes. Blackmail or no blackmail, I still feel it's most likely to be him. We'll see what Colgate can make out of the alibi. In the meantime, I've got the chambermaid waiting to be interviewed.'

The chambermaid, Gladys Narracott, was a woman of thirty, efficient and intelligent. Her answers came quickly.

Captain Marshall had come up to his room not long after 10.30 am, she said. He had asked her to be as quick as possible. She had not seen him come back but had heard the typewriter later. She guessed that was at about five minutes to eleven. She was then in Mr and Mrs Redfern's room. She moved on to Miss Darnley's room at the end of the corridor, but she couldn't hear the typewriter from there. That was a bit after eleven o'clock. She remembered hearing Leathercombe Church strike the hour. At quarter past eleven she had gone downstairs for her cup of tea.

In answer to the Chief Constable's question, she explained that during the time she was in Miss Darnley's room, she hadn't heard anyone pass the door or go out by the stairs to the rocks. But she believed she wouldn't have heard anyone moving quietly.

Weston said, 'Hmm, well, I think that's all at present.' He looked at Poirot.

Poirot leaned forward: 'When you cleaned Miss Linda Marshall's room this morning, did you clean the fire grate?'

'There wasn't anything to clean, sir. There hadn't been a fire lit,' replied Gladys Narracott.

'And there was nothing in the grate itself?'

'No, sir.'

'What time did you clean her room?'

'About quarter past nine, sir, when she'd gone down to breakfast.'

'Did she come up to her room after breakfast, do you know?'

'Yes, sir. She came up at about quarter to ten.'

Poirot nodded. 'There is another thing I want to know,' he said. 'Who swam before breakfast this morning?'

'Well, sir, Captain Marshall and Mr Redfern were the only ones this morning. They always go down for an early swim.'

'Did you see them?'

'No, sir, but their wet swimming things were hanging over the balcony as usual.'

'Miss Linda Marshall did not swim this morning?'

'No, sir. All her swimsuits were dry.'

'Ah,' said Poirot. 'That is what I wanted to know.' Then he asked, 'I wonder if you have noticed whether a bottle is missing from any of the rooms?'

'A bottle, sir? What kind of bottle?'

'Unfortunately, I do not know. But would you notice if one had gone?'

Gladys said honestly, 'Not from Mrs Marshall's room, sir. She has so many. I'm not sure about Miss Darnley. But from the other rooms, yes, I would, sir. I mean, if I were to look especially.'

'Perhaps you would go and look now, then.'

'Certainly, sir.'

She left the room.

Weston looked at Poirot. He said, 'What's all this about?'

'I have an orderly mind, which is concerned with small details,' replied Poirot. 'This morning, Miss Brewster was swimming off the rocks before breakfast, and she says that a bottle was thrown from above and nearly hit her. *Eh bien* – so, I want to know who threw that bottle and why.'

'My dear man, anyone may have thrown a bottle away.'

'Not at all. Now I ask you, if you have an empty bottle on your dressing table or in your bathroom, what do you do with it? You drop it into the bin. You do not take the trouble to go out onto your balcony and throw it into the sea! No, you would only do that *if you did not want anyone to see that particular bottle.*'

Weston stared at him.

'What do you think was in that bottle?'

'I do not know. That is why I am interested.'

Gladys Narracott came back.

'I'm sorry, sir, but I can't find anything missing,' she said.

'Thank you,' said Poirot. 'Now, are you sure there is nothing at all you have forgotten to tell us?'

'About Mrs Marshall, sir?'

'About anything unusual, odd, peculiar – something that has made you say to yourself or to one of your colleagues, "That is funny!"?'

Gladys said doubtfully, 'Well, not the sort of thing you would mean, sir.'

Poirot said, 'Never mind what I mean. You do not know what I mean. It is true, then, that you have said to yourself or to a colleague today, "That is funny!"?'

Gladys shook her head and said, 'It was nothing, really. Just a bath being run. And I did say to Elsie, downstairs, that it was funny, somebody having a bath round about twelve o'clock.'

'Whose bath? Who had a bath?'

'I don't know, sir. We heard the water going down the pipes, that's all.'

'Are you sure that it was a bath?' asked Poirot.

'Oh, quite sure, sir,' replied Gladys. 'You can't make a mistake about the sound of bath water running away.'

As Gladys Narracott was leaving, a policeman knocked at the door.

'It's Miss Darnley, sir,' he said to Weston. 'She'd like to see you again for a minute. There's something she forgot to tell you, she says.'

Weston said, 'We're coming down – now.'

◆ ◆ ◆

The first person they saw downstairs was Inspector Colgate. He looked unhappy.

He followed Colonel Weston and Hercule Poirot into Mrs Castle's office.

Colgate said, 'There's not a doubt, sir. The typing couldn't have been done in under an hour. And look at this letter.'

He held it out.

'My dear Marshall,

Sorry to worry you on your holiday but there's an entirely unexpected situation with the Burley and Tender contracts…'

'Dated the 24th,' Colgate added. 'And by the contents, it was clearly impossible for Marshall to write his answer before he received that letter.'

'Hmm,' said Weston. 'That seems to give Marshall his alibi.' He added, 'I've got to see Miss Darnley again now. She's waiting.'

◆ ◆ ◆

'I'm sorry. Probably this isn't worth bothering about. But you forget things, don't you?' said Rosamund.

'Yes, Miss Darnley?' said Weston.

'It's simply that I told you I spent the morning lying out on Sunny Ledge. I forgot that I came back to the hotel once. I'd forgotten my sunglasses. My eyes got tired and I decided to go in and get them. And I looked in on Ken— Captain Marshall. I heard his typewriter going and I thought it was so stupid of him to stay indoors typing on such a lovely day. I thought I'd tell him to come out.'

'And what did Captain Marshall say?'

Rosamund smiled.

'Well, when I opened the door he was so focused on his typing, and looking so serious and concentrated, that I just went away quietly. I don't think he even saw me.'

'And what time was that, Miss Darnley?'

'Just about twenty past eleven. I noticed the clock downstairs as I went out again.'

◆ ◆ ◆

'So Captain Marshall can't be a suspect,' said the Inspector after Rosamund had left. 'He says he spent that hour typing in his room, and it's clear he *was* typing in his room.'

Poirot said thoughtfully, 'I am wondering why Miss Darnley suddenly decided to give us this extra evidence.'

'You think that it isn't just a question of "forgetting"?' asked Colgate. He considered for a minute: 'She was careful to say Captain Marshall didn't see her.'

Poirot murmured, 'Yes, I noticed that.'

Weston said, 'I think we'd better see if Captain Marshall had enough time to get across the island. Find someone to time how long it takes to get from the hotel to the top of the Pixy Cove ladder. Same thing with the ladder itself. And check the time it takes to go on a float from the swimming beach to the cove.'

Colgate nodded: 'Yes, sir.'

'I think I'll go along to the cove now too,' the Chief Constable decided. 'I want to see if they've found anything there. Then there's Pixy's Cave. We should see if there are any traces of a man waiting in there. We could take Redfern with us – he told us about it. What about you, Monsieur Poirot? Will you come?'

Poirot hesitated.

'Me, I am like Miss Brewster and Mrs Redfern – I do not like to descend long ladders.'

Weston said, 'You can go by boat.'

Poirot sighed.

'My stomach is not happy on the sea.'

'Nonsense, man, it's a beautiful, calm day. You can't let us down.'

At that moment, Mrs Castle looked round the door.

'Excuse me, but Mr Lane has just returned,' she said. 'I thought you might like to know.'

'Ah yes, thanks, Mrs Castle. We'll see him right away.'

◆ ◆ ◆

Stephen Lane entered the room with his usual energy.

'I'm the Chief Constable, Mr Lane,' Colonel Weston said. 'I suppose you've been told what's happened?'

'Oh yes. Terrible… Terrible…' His thin frame shook. 'Ever since I arrived here, I've been aware of the forces of evil close by.' His eager eyes looked at Hercule Poirot. 'You remember, Monsieur Poirot? Our conversation about evil?'

'Mr Lane, let's stick to the point,' Weston said. 'My job is to clear up a case of murder.'

'Then in what way can I help?'

'First, Mr Lane, tell me where you've been and what you've done today.'

'Of course. I started off early on one of my usual hikes. Today I went to St Petrock-in-the-Combe, about seven miles from here – a very pleasant walk up and down the hills and valleys.'

'Did you meet anyone on your walk?'

'Not to speak to. A cart passed me, and a couple of boys on bicycles and some cows. However,' he smiled, 'I wrote my name in the visitor's book at the church. You'll find it there.'

'You didn't see anyone at the church?'

Stephen Lane shook his head: 'There was no one nearby.'

Weston said pleasantly, 'Now, is there anything you know about the dead woman that could give us an idea as to who murdered her?'

Stephen Lane said, 'All I can tell you is this – that I knew as soon as I saw her that Arlena Marshall was evil. Now she has been <u>struck down</u> in her <u>wickedness</u>!'

Poirot said, 'Not struck down – strangled! Strangled, Mr Lane, by a pair of human hands.'

Stephen Lane's own hands trembled. His voice was low and emotional, 'That's horrible – horrible... Must you say it like that?'

'It is the simple truth. Do you have any idea, Mr Lane, whose hands those were?'

Lane shook his head: 'I know nothing – nothing...'

Weston got up: 'Well, we must go to the cove.'

'Can – can I come with you?' Lane asked.

'Certainly,' said Poirot before Weston could refuse. 'Accompany me there in a boat, Mr Lane. We leave immediately.'

CHAPTER 9

For the second time that day, Patrick Redfern was rowing a boat into Pixy Cove. The other people in the boat were Hercule Poirot, very pale with a hand to his stomach, and Stephen Lane. Colonel Weston had gone by land. When the boat arrived, Weston and two other policemen were already on the beach.

One of the policemen was saying to Weston, 'I've been over every centimetre of the beach, sir. It's all here – everything I've found.'

A collection of objects was laid out on a rock. A pair of scissors, an empty cigarette packet, five bottle tops, a number of used matches, three pieces of string, a bit of a smashed tobacco pipe, four buttons and an empty bottle of sunbathing oil.

'Hmm,' Weston said. 'The bottle's been here some time. So have most of the other things, I would say. The scissors are new, though. Bright and shiny. Where were they?'

'By the bottom of the ladder, sir.'

'Hmm. Is there any way of knowing who they belong to?'

'No, sir. They're an ordinary pair of nail scissors. The pipe's good quality, though – expensive.'

Weston turned to Redfern. 'Now then, man, where's this cave of yours?' he asked.

Patrick Redfern was staring down at the beach, as though he was seeing the body that was no longer there.

He said in a low voice, 'I'm glad they've taken her away...'

Stephen Lane asked, 'Where was she found?'

The policeman said cheerfully, 'Where you're standing, sir.'

Lane moved quickly aside. He hurried after Redfern as he led the way to a mass of rocks against the side of the cliff. Two big rocks had a narrow gap between them.

Weston said, 'It doesn't look as though a man could squeeze through.'

'It can just be done, sir.'

Weston pushed himself into the gap. It was not as narrow as it looked. Inside, the space widened with room to stand up and move about. Poirot and Lane joined the Chief Constable.

Weston said, 'Well, well! You'd never suspect it from the outside.' He shone a powerful torch over the floor.

Poirot was smelling the air.

Noticing this, Weston said, 'The air is fresh.'

But to Poirot the air was more than fresh. It was <u>scented</u>. He knew two people who used that perfume…

Weston said, 'I don't see anything.'

Poirot looked up at a ledge above his head.

'You are the tallest of us, Monsieur Lane. Could you make sure there is nothing on that ledge?' he asked.

Lane reached up, 'Oh, there's a box up here.'

Soon, they were out in the sunshine examining a dark-green tin box with the word *Sandwiches* on it.

One of the policemen opened the lid with his handkerchief. The box was filled with <u>glittering</u> stones that reflected the light.

'Diamonds, sir!' said the policeman excitedly.

◆ ◆ ◆

'So now we have a third possibility,' Colonel Weston complained.

They were meeting at the hotel again, in Mrs Castle's office.

'I'm afraid so,' Inspector Colgate confirmed, 'and a nasty one. Apparently an armed gang robbed one of the diamond-cutting firms in Antwerp recently. One man was shot dead and another was badly injured. We knew the diamonds were coming into the country, but we've been watching the east coast ports – nothing this far west.'

The Chief Constable said, 'So, the dead woman may have been in the gang. Or she may have run into the business accidentally – and was silenced. We'll need to—'

He stopped as the door was opened, and Mr Horace Blatt came into the room.

Blatt was looking hot. He was wiping the sweat from his forehead. His big voice filled the small room.

'I just got back and heard the news! Are you the Chief Constable? They told me you were in here. My name's Blatt – Horace Blatt. I don't suppose there's any way I can help? I've been out in my boat since early this morning. I missed everything! I heard Mrs Marshall was murdered. Strangled at Pixy Cove, eh?' Blatt said, excitedly. 'Very nasty. Any idea who did it?'

Weston said, 'It's us who ask the questions, Mr Blatt.'

'Sorry – sorry. Go ahead.'

'You went out sailing this morning. At what time?'

'At quarter to ten. I went towards Plymouth. There wasn't much wind so I didn't get far.'

Weston asked, 'About the Marshalls – do you know anything that might help us?'

'Well, in my opinion, it was a crime of passion!' replied Blatt. 'The beautiful Arlena had her boy! And if you ask me, Marshall found out about it.'

'Do you have any evidence for that?'

'I saw him give young Redfern a look once or twice. Marshall looks very gentle and quiet – but he's the sort of man who could lose control.'

Poirot said, 'Mr Blatt, we believe Mrs Marshall went to Pixy Cove to meet someone. Do you have any idea who?'

Mr Blatt winked: 'Redfern!'

'It was not Mr Redfern.'

Mr Blatt was surprised: 'Then I don't know...'

He wiped his forehead once more.

When he had gone out, Weston said, 'And what do we think of Mr Blatt?'

Poirot said, 'He is nervous!'

♦ ◆ ♦

'I've got those times worked out,' Inspector Colgate announced. 'From the hotel to the top of the Pixy Cove ladder: three minutes. That's running really fast.'

Colonel Weston raised his eyebrows: 'That's quicker than I thought.'

'Down the ladder to the beach: one and three-quarter minutes. Up the ladder: two minutes. Walking and taking the ladder at a normal speed, it takes more or less a quarter of an hour.'

Weston pulled at his moustache: 'What I'd—'

There was a tap on the door. It was Captain Marshall.

'Can you tell me when I can arrange the funeral?' he asked.

'The inquest will be the day after tomorrow, Captain Marshall. We won't know anything until after that.'

'Thank you.'

Colgate said, 'Excuse me, sir, allow me to return these.' He handed over the letters.

Kenneth Marshall smiled, 'I hope I am no longer a suspect.'

Weston said pleasantly, 'No, Captain Marshall. Miss Darnley came to your room at twenty minutes past eleven. You were so busy typing that you didn't see her.'

Kenneth Marshall's face became still.

'Did Miss Darnley say that?' He paused. 'She's wrong, though she may not be aware of the fact. I saw her in the mirror.'

Poirot said, 'But you did not interrupt your typing?'

'I wanted to finish it.'

Kenneth Marshall nodded and went out.

Weston said with a sigh, 'There goes our most hopeful suspect – innocent!'

Colgate shook his head.

'Believe me, sir, this diamond gang is the answer to the whole business.'

CHAPTER 10

The public inquest was over for now.

Rosamund Darnley joined Captain Marshall. She said in a low voice, 'That wasn't so bad, was it, Ken?'

Marshall did not answer. Perhaps he was thinking of the staring eyes and the fingers pointing at him! Thinking of the stories that had appeared in the morning papers, with his words changed – they were not what he'd really said. Thinking of the cameras that did not stop clicking. He heard the familiar sound and half-turned. He saw saw a young man nodding cheerfully, his job done.

Rosamund murmured, *'Captain Marshall and a friend leaving after the inquest.*

'You've got to face it, Ken! Not just Arlena's death – but all this. The staring and gossiping, the nonsense in the papers. You can't just fade into the background. You're like a tiger against a white cloth for everyone to see. The husband of the murdered woman!'

'Please, Rosamund—'

She said gently, 'My dear, I'm trying to be good for you!'

They walked for a few steps in silence. Then Marshall said, 'I know you are – and I'm grateful, Rosamund.'

They came to the causeway. Opposite them, beautiful in the sunlight, was the island. They walked across to it.

On the other side of the causeway, Linda came down to meet them. Her young face had deep black shadows under her eyes.

She said nervously, 'What happened?'

Her father said <u>abruptly</u>, 'There'll be another inquest in a fortnight.'

'That means they— they haven't decided what happened?'

'Yes, my dear child. More evidence is needed.' Marshall's lips closed tightly. He went into the hotel.

As Rosamund Darnley was about to follow him, Linda said, 'Rosamund!'

Rosamund saw the girl's unhappy face. She linked her arm through Linda's, and together they walked along the path that led to the end of the island.

Rosamund said gently, 'Linda, I know it's a terrible shock, but it's no use thinking about it. And it can only be the horror of her death that's worrying you. You didn't actually like Arlena.'

She felt the girl's body shake.

Rosamund went on, 'You can get over shock by just not letting yourself think about it.'

Linda said, 'No, you don't understand – and Christine doesn't either! Both of you have been nice to me, but you can't understand what I'm feeling. If you knew what I know...'

Rosamund stopped dead. Her body tensed. She gripped Linda's arm. It hurt.

'Be careful, Linda,' she said. 'Be very careful.'

Linda's face had turned white.

'I am very careful – *all the time.*'

Rosamund said in a very serious voice, 'Put the whole business out of your mind, Linda. Forget everything and live in the future. And above all, say nothing.'

Linda tried to move away from her: 'You— you seem to know all about it?'

Rosamund said, 'No, I don't know anything! In my opinion, a wandering madman killed Arlena. The police will have to accept that in the end.'

Linda said, 'I've got to say one thing. My mother – she was tried for murder. And then Father married her. That looks, doesn't it, as though Father didn't think murder was always wrong?'

Rosamund said quickly, 'Don't! Your father has an alibi the police can't break. He's safe. Do you understand? He *couldn't* have done it.'

The girl gave a long sigh.

Rosamund said, 'Forget everything!'

Linda said with sudden violence. '*I'll never forget!*'

She turned and ran back to the hotel.

◆ ◆ ◆

'There is something I want to know, Madame Redfern,' said Poirot.

'Yes?'

Hercule Poirot noted the way Christine Redfern's eyes followed her husband as he walked up and down the terrace outside the bar. But he had no interest in that – he wanted information.

He said, 'Yes, madame. It was a phrase of yours which caught my attention. You said you went into Linda Marshall's room on the morning of the crime, that she was not there but then she returned. The Chief Constable asked you where she had been.'

'Yes, and I said she had been swimming,' Christine said impatiently.

'Ah, but you did not. Your words were, "she said she had been swimming." It is not the same! Linda Marshall was wearing a swimsuit and a towel and yet you did not assume she had been swimming. Why?'

Christine looked up, her attention now focused entirely on Poirot. 'That's clever of you,' she said. 'It's true, I remember... I was surprised when Linda said she'd been swimming.'

'But why, madame?'

'It was the parcel in her hand.'

'A parcel? Do you know what was in it?'

'Oh yes, I do. The string broke and it all fell on the floor. It was candles. I helped her to pick them up.'

'Ah,' said Poirot. 'Candles.'

Christine stared at him: 'You seem excited, Monsieur Poirot.'

As an answer, Poirot took out a small book. He showed her the title.

Death Cults, Barbarian Rituals and Untraceable Poisons[12].

Christine said, 'I don't understand. What does all this mean?'

Poirot said in a very serious tone, 'It may mean a good deal, madame... One more question. Did you have a bath that morning before you went to play tennis?'

Christine stared again:

'No.'

◆ ◆ ◆

Hercule Poirot tapped on the door of Captain Marshall's room. Inside, he heard the sound of a typewriter.

'Come in!' called Marshall.

Poirot entered. Marshall was typing at a table between the windows. He did not turn round, but his eyes met Poirot's in the mirror on the wall.

'What is it?' he said, annoyed by the interruption.

'There is one question I would like to ask you,' said Poirot.

Marshall said, 'I'm sick of answering questions.'

'Mine is a simple one,' Poirot said. 'On the morning of your wife's death, did you have a bath before you went to play tennis?'

'A bath? No, of course I didn't!'

'Thank you,' Poirot said, gently closing the door.

♦ ◆ ♦

'So it's my turn, is it?' Rosamund Darnley said as Poirot approached her.

'I do not understand,' lied Poirot.

She laughed: 'I've been watching you make your inquiries. Now it's my turn.'

Poirot sat down beside her. They were on Sunny Ledge. The sea was a deep green.

'You are very intelligent, mademoiselle. May I ask you a question?'

'Certainly.'

She faced him, ready. But the question was an unexpected one.

'When you changed into your tennis dress that morning, did you have a bath?'

Rosamund stared at him:

'Monsieur Poirot, are you mad?'

'No, I am most definitely not.'

'Well, no, I didn't have a bath.'

'Ha!' said Poirot. 'So nobody had a bath. That is very interesting.'

'But why would anyone have a bath?'

'Why, indeed?' Poirot smiled. Then he smelled the air. 'May I say, mademoiselle, that the perfume you use is lovely. Gabrielle No. 8, I think?'

'Yes, I always use it.'

'Mmm, so did Mrs Marshall.' Poirot continued, 'You sat here, mademoiselle, on the morning of the crime. Are you sure you did not go down to Pixy Cove and enter the cave there?'

Rosamund stared at him: 'Are you asking me if I killed Arlena Marshall?'

'No, I am asking you if you went into Pixy's Cave.'

'I don't even know where it is!'

'On the day of the crime, mademoiselle, somebody had been in that cave who used Gabrielle No. 8.'

Rosamund said quickly, 'You've just said, Monsieur Poirot, that Arlena Marshall used Gabrielle No. 8 too. So presumably *she* went into the cave.'

'Why would she? It is dark and uncomfortable.'

Rosamund said impatiently, 'Don't ask me. I never left *this* place.'

'Except for when you went up to the hotel to Captain Marshall's room,' Poirot reminded her.

'Yes, of course.'

Poirot said, 'And you were wrong, mademoiselle – Captain Marshall did see you.'

Rosamund said, 'Kenneth saw me? Did— did he say so?'

Poirot nodded: 'He saw you, mademoiselle, in the mirror.'

'Oh!'

Inspector Colgate was reporting to the Chief Constable: 'About Mrs Marshall's money, sir – I've been talking to her lawyers. Of the fifty thousand pounds she got from old Erskine, only fifteen thousand are left.'

The Chief Constable whistled in surprise. 'Whew, what's happened to the rest?' he asked.

'Blackmail, I think,' replied the Inspector.

Weston nodded.

'And the blackmailer must be one of three men in this hotel. Have you got any new information about them?'

'Nothing definite, sir. Major Barry's a retired army man, as he says. He lives in a small flat, receives a small pension from the army and has a few investments which make him some money, but not much. However, he's paid various other large amounts of money into his bank account in the last year. When I asked him about them, he said that he and a friend from his army days have done a few business deals together with people they know from their time in India.'

'Mmm, it's hard to prove that's a lie, then,' the Chief Constable said.

Colgate went on. 'Next, Stephen Lane. He used to live at St Helen's, Whiteridge, in Surrey. Then, just over a year ago, he went into a psychiatric hospital. He was there for a year.'

'Interesting,' said Weston.

'Yes, sir. His doctor says he believed that some women carry evil within them.'

'Hmm,' said Weston. 'That fits the murder but not the blackmail.'

'No, sir. He has some money of his own, but no sudden money coming into his bank account.'

Weston nodded: 'And the third man?'

'Horace Blatt? He's suspicious! He's involved in some <u>shady</u> business deals. He's been making lots of money for years.'

'Is he a blackmailer by profession, do you think?'

'Either that, sir, or he's involved with the robbery gang. By the way, I checked up on the writer of that letter we found in the victim's room – the one signed J.N. He's in China sure enough. It's the same man that Miss Brewster was telling us about.'

'And what about our Belgian colleague, Monsieur Poirot?' Weston asked. 'Does he know all you've told me?'

Colgate said with a smile, 'He's an odd man, isn't he? He asked me about other cases in the last three years where the victim was strangled.'

Weston sat up.

'Did he? Now I wonder—' he paused. 'When did you say Stephen Lane went into that hospital?'

'A year ago last Easter, sir.'

Weston was thinking deeply. He said, 'There *was* a case – the body of a young woman was found near Bagshot. She was going to meet her husband and never turned up. And there was what the papers called the Lonely <u>Copse</u> Mystery. Both cases happened in Surrey.'

His eyes met those of the Inspector.

Colgate said, 'Surrey? My word, sir – it fits, doesn't it?'

◆ ◆ ◆

Hercule Poirot sat on the grass at the top of the island, looking out over the sea. To his left was the steel ladder that led down to Pixy Cove.

He nodded his head.

The pieces of his puzzle were fitting into position, each fact into its place. But there must be no <u>loose ends</u>.

He looked down at the piece of paper in his hands.

Nellie Parsons – found strangled in a lonely copse. No murderer ever discovered.

Alice Corrigan.

He was reading the details of Alice Corrigan's death when Inspector Colgate came across the grass and sat down beside him.

Poirot liked Inspector Colgate. He liked his clever eyes and his slow manner.

The Inspector glanced down at the papers in Poirot's hand and said, 'I don't mind telling you, Monsieur Poirot, that I might not have thought about those cases if you hadn't asked for them.' He paused, then continued, 'I've spoken to the Surrey police about the Alice Corrigan case – I wanted to get all the details.'

'Tell me, my friend,' said Poirot. 'I am very interested in the details – about anything not in these reports.'

The inspector replied, 'Alice Corrigan was found strangled in Caesar's Grove on Blackridge Heath – not ten miles from Marley Copse where Nellie Parsons was found. Both places are within twelve miles of Whiteridge, where Mr Lane lived. The Surrey police didn't at first connect her death with that of Nellie Parsons. That's because they'd decided the husband was guilty. He was a bit of what the press calls a "mystery man" – not much was known about who he was or where he came from. She'd married him against her family's wishes.'

Poirot nodded.

'But,' continued Colgate, 'when it came down to facts, it was clear that it wasn't the husband. The body was discovered by a <u>hiker</u>. She was a reliable witness – a P.E. teacher at a school in Lancashire. She noted the time when she found the body – 4.15 pm – and gave her opinion that the woman had been dead for not more than ten minutes. That fitted with the police doctor's view when he examined the body.

Now, from three o'clock to ten past four, Edward Corrigan, the husband, was on a train from London. Four other people were in the carriage with him. From the station he took the local bus – with two of the other passengers from the train. He got off at the Pine Ridge Café where he'd arranged to meet his wife for tea. The time then was 4.25 pm. Once the husband was proved to be innocent, naturally they connected Alice's death with that of Nellie Parsons – they decided the same man was responsible for both crimes, but they never caught him!'

He paused and then he said: 'And now, here's a third woman strangled – and a certain gentleman right here.'

Poirot said, 'Tell me, Inspector Colgate, if you suspected someone of telling lies – many, many lies – but you had no proof, what would you do?'

Colgate considered:

'It's difficult. But they're bound to make a mistake in the end.'

Poirot nodded.

'Yes, that is true. You see, I *think* certain statements we have heard are lies, but I cannot *know* they are lies. But it is perhaps possible to make a test of one particular lie. And if that were proved to be a lie – well, then we would know that all the rest were lies, too!'

Colgate looked at him:

'If you'll excuse me asking, what made you think about these cases?'

'You have a word in your language,' Poirot said. 'Slick. This crime seemed a very slick crime! It made me wonder if, perhaps, it was not a first attempt. So I said to myself, let us examine past crimes of a similar kind.'

'You mean using the same method of death, sir?'

'I mean more than that, Inspector Colgate. Do you not notice one striking similarity in these crimes?'

Colgate thought about it. He said at last.

'No, sir. Unless it's that in each case the husband has got a cast-iron alibi.'

Poirot said softly, 'Ah, so you *have* noticed that.'

'Ah, Poirot,' said Colonel Weston as Hercule Poirot entered the room. 'Come in. You're just the man I want. I've decided what to do next. But I'd like your opinion before I act.'

Poirot said, 'Tell me, *mon ami* – my friend.'

The Chief Constable went on, 'I've decided to hand the case over to Scotland Yard[13]. It seems clear to me that Pixy's Cave was being used for diamond smuggling.'

Poirot nodded: 'I agree.'

'Good man. And I'm thinking our smuggler is Horace Blatt.'

Again Poirot agreed, 'That, too, seems true.'

'I see our minds have both worked the same way. I think Blatt sailed out to an agreed spot, was met by another boat and the diamonds were handed over. Then Blatt lands at Pixy Cove and hides them in the cave. Somebody else was supposed to pick the package up from there later. Then Arlena Marshall arrives on her float and sees Blatt going into the cave with the box. She asks him about it, and he kills her.

'Of course, I know that you and Colgate have other ideas. And I'm bound to admit there may be something in it. But as I say, I think it best to hand the case over to Scotland Yard. You agree that's the wise thing to do, eh?'

Poirot was thoughtful. He said at last, 'It may be.'

'Oh come on, Poirot, have you got an idea you want to share, or haven't you?'

Poirot said seriously, 'If I have, I am not sure that I can prove it.'

'Well, what do you feel should be done about that, Poirot?'

Poirot seemed lost in thought. At last he said, 'I know what I would like to do.'

'And what's that?' asked the Chief Constable.

'I would like to go for a picnic.'

CHAPTER 12

'A *picnic*, Monsieur Poirot?' said Emily Brewster.

She stared at Poirot as though he were mad.

Poirot said, 'Indeed, it seems a good idea to me. We need some everyday activity to restore life to normal. I would like to see the countryside, and the weather is good. It will cheer everybody up!'

Everyone was at first <u>dubious</u>, but then admitted it might not be a bad idea after all.

Mr Blatt was determined to be the life and soul of the event. Besides him, there were Emily Brewster, the Redferns, Stephen Lane, the Gardeners, Rosamund Darnley and Linda.

Captain Marshall was not invited.

Major Barry refused to come. He did not like picnics. 'There are always lots of baskets to carry,' he complained.

The group met at ten o'clock. Three cars had been ordered.

At the last minute, Rosamund Darnley came downstairs, looking concerned. 'Linda's not coming,' she said. 'She says she's got a headache.'

Poirot cried, 'But it will do her good to come. Persuade her, mademoiselle.'

Rosamund said, 'It's no good. She's determined. I've given her some headache tablets and she's gone to bed.'

She hesitated, then said, 'Perhaps I won't go, either.'

Christine Redfern said, 'No. I'll stay with Linda. I don't mind at all.'

Poirot said, 'No, no, you must both come. If she has a headache, she is better alone. Come, let us go.'

The three cars drove off. Mr Blatt was loud and cheerful. They went first to the famous Pixy's Cave on Sheepstor. It had been famous since the 1800s – and the rocks at the entrance to the cave were a lot more dramatic than the rocks at Pixy Cove. It was a lot of fun looking for the cave entrance and at last finding it.

It was difficult going over the big rocks. Poirot watched while Christine Redfern jumped lightly from stone to stone, her husband never far from her. Rosamund Darnley and Emily Brewster joined in, as did Stephen Lane, his long thin figure running among the rocks. Mr Blatt shouted encouragement and took photographs of them all.

The Gardeners and Poirot remained sitting by the road while Mrs Gardener's voice went on in a pleasant <u>monologue</u>.

'—and what I've always felt, Monsieur Poirot – and Mr Gardener agrees with me – is that photographs can be very annoying. Unless they are taken among friends. That Mr Blatt – he just comes right up to everyone and takes pictures and, as I said to Mr Gardener, that really is awful. That's what I said, Odell, wasn't it?'

'Yes, darling.'

'That group photograph he took of us all sitting on the beach. Well, he should have asked first. As it was, Miss Brewster was just getting up, and it certainly makes her look a peculiar shape.'

'I'll say it does,' said Mr Gardener with a smile.

'And there's Mr Blatt, giving copies to everybody without so much as asking first. He gave one to you, Monsieur Poirot, I noticed.'

Poirot nodded: 'I value that photograph very much.'

At this moment the discovery of Pixy's Cave was shouted from below.

The party now drove on, under Hercule Poirot's directions, to a spot where a short walk from the car down a hill led to a lovely spot by a small river. There was a narrow wooden bridge over the river. Poirot and Mr Gardener helped Mrs Gardener to cross it to a perfect place for a picnic lunch.

Mrs Gardener continued talking about her feelings after crossing the bridge, then she sank down on the grass. Suddenly there was a cry. The others had run across the bridge easily enough, but Emily Brewster was standing in the middle of it, her eyes shut, <u>swaying</u>.

Poirot and Patrick Redfern rushed to the rescue. Emily Brewster was embarrassed.

'Thanks, thanks,' she said, 'Sorry. I was never good at crossing running water. I get dizzy. It's very stupid.'

Lunch was spread out and the picnic began.

Everybody was surprised to find how much they enjoyed the day. Here, with the running water and the soft smell of grass in the air, the world of murder and police inquiries seemed as though it had never existed.

It was a grateful party of people who packed up the picnic baskets and thanked Hercule Poirot for his good idea.

♦ ◆ ♦

On their arrival back on the island, the chambermaid, Gladys Narracott, came hurrying out of the hotel. She approached Christine Redfern.

'Madam, I'm worried about Miss Marshall. I took her some tea and I couldn't get her to wake up.'

Poirot was at her side in a moment: 'We will go up and see.'

They hurried up to Linda's room. Her face was an unhealthy colour and she was barely breathing. Poirot felt for her <u>pulse</u>. There was an envelope on the table addressed to him.

A frightened cry came from Christine Redfern.

Captain Marshall came quickly into the room.

Poirot said, 'Get a doctor – quick!'

He ripped open the letter. Inside were a few lines in Linda's schoolgirl handwriting.

I think this is the best way out. Ask Father to try and forgive me. I killed Arlena. I thought I would be happy – but I'm not. I am very sorry for everything.

♦ ◆ ♦

They were all downstairs in the hotel – Marshall, the Redferns, Rosamund Darnley and Hercule Poirot.

They were silent – waiting…

The door opened and Dr Neasdon came in. He said, 'I've done all I can. She may recover – but I have to tell you there's not much hope.'

Marshall, his face tense, his eyes cold, asked, 'How did she get the drugs?'

Christine said almost in a whisper, 'I gave her my sleeping tablets. It was the night after the murder happened. Linda told me she couldn't sleep. She— I remember her saying—"Will one be enough?" – and I said yes, that they were very strong – that I'd been told never to take more than two at most.'

Dr Neasdon nodded. 'She wanted to make sure they worked,' he said. 'She took six.'

Christine started crying again. She said in despair, 'She's dying – and it's my fault.'

Colonel Weston came in: 'What's all this I hear?'

Dr Neasdon handed the note to the Chief Constable. He read it: '*What?* But this is nonsense! It's impossible. Isn't it, Poirot?'

Poirot said sadly, 'No, I am afraid not.'

Christine Redfern said, 'But I was with her, Monsieur Poirot. Up to quarter to twelve. I told the police that.'

Poirot said, 'Your evidence gave her an alibi – yes. But your evidence was based on Linda Marshall's own watch. You do not *know* that it was quarter to twelve when you left her – you only know that *she told you it was.*'

He turned to Marshall.

'I must describe to you what I found in your daughter's room after the murder. In the grate there was melted wax, some burnt hair, pieces of cardboard and paper and a pin. I also found a book about <u>death rituals</u>. It opened at a page that described methods of causing death by making a figure in wax to represent the victim. This was then slowly burnt till it melted – or alternatively you would put a pin in the heart of the wax figure. The death of the victim would follow.

'I heard from Mrs Redfern that Linda had been out early that morning and bought a packet of candles. I have no doubt that Linda made a figure out of the candle wax – possibly adding a small piece of Arlena's red hair. Then I believe she stabbed it to the heart with a pin and finally melted the figure away by lighting pieces of cardboard under it.

'It was silly and childish, but it showed her desire to kill. Could Linda Marshall have actually killed her stepmother? At first it seemed that she had a perfect alibi – but as I have pointed out, the time evidence was supplied by Linda herself. She could easily have said the time was a quarter of an hour later than it really was.'

Marshall said, 'I don't believe that Linda killed Arlena. It's ridiculous!'

Poirot said, 'Do you believe that letter, then, is a <u>forgery</u>?'

Marshall held out his hand for the letter and Weston gave it to him. Marshall studied it, then he shook his head. 'No,' he said. 'Linda did write this.'

Poirot said, 'Then there are only two explanations. Either she wrote it knowing herself to be the murderer, or... or she wrote it to protect someone whom she feared was suspected.'

Kenneth Marshall said slowly, 'You mean me?'

'It is possible, is it not?' asked Poirot.

Marshall considered for a moment, then said quietly, 'No. Linda knew the police had accepted my alibi.'

Poirot said, 'And suppose it was not that she thought you were suspected, but that she *knew* you were guilty.'

Marshall stared at him: 'I've just told you—'

'Yes, yes – I agree it is impossible that you killed your wife – if you were acting alone. But if someone had helped you?'

The quiet man was <u>roused</u> at last. He got up from his chair. His voice was low, his eyes hard and angry: 'What do you mean?'

Poirot said, 'I mean that this crime was not committed by just one person. There were two people. True, you could not have typed that letter and at the same time gone to the cove – but there was time for you to write down that letter in notes, and for someone else to type it in your room while you were absent committing the murder.'

Hercule Poirot looked towards Rosamund Darnley: 'Miss Darnley states that she left Sunny Ledge at quarter past eleven and saw you typing in your room. But at about that time, Mr Gardener went up to the hotel to fetch a ball of wool for his wife. He did not meet Miss Darnley or see her. That is odd. It looks as though either Miss Darnley never left Sunny Ledge, or else she had left it much earlier and was in your room, typing.

'And another point,' continued Poirot. 'You stated that when Miss Darnley looked into your room, you saw her in the mirror. But on the day of the murder, your typewriter and papers were all on the writing desk across in the corner of the room, whereas the mirror was between the windows. So that statement was a lie. Later, you moved your typewriter to the table under the mirror to prove your story – but it was too late. I knew you and Miss Darnley had lied about seeing one another.'

Rosamund Darnley spoke. Her voice was low and clear: 'How clever you are!'

Hercule Poirot raised his voice: 'But not as clever as the man who killed Arlena Marshall! Think back for a moment. Who did I believe – who did everybody believe – that Arlena Marshall had gone to meet that morning? Patrick Redfern. She did not go to meet a blackmailer. I met her on the beach that morning – her face told me it was a lover she was going to meet – or thought she was going to meet.

'Yes, I was sure that Arlena Marshall was going to meet Patrick Redfern. But a minute later Patrick Redfern appeared on the beach and was obviously looking for her. So what then?'

Patrick Redfern said with quiet anger in his voice, 'Somebody must have sent her a note arranging to meet her – and used my name.'

Poirot said, 'You were obviously upset and surprised when she did not appear. Almost too obviously, perhaps. It is my theory, Mr Redfern, that she went to Pixy Cove to meet you, and that she did meet you, and that you killed her there as you had planned to do.'

Redfern said, 'But I was with you on the beach until I went with Miss Brewster to Pixy Cove and found her dead!'

Poirot said, 'But no. Arlena Marshall was *not* dead when you got to the beach. She was waiting, hidden in the cave until it was safe to come out. You killed her after Miss Brewster had gone off in the boat to fetch the police.'

'But the body! Miss Brewster and I both saw the body.'

'You saw *a* body – yes. But not a dead body. It was the *live* body of the woman who helped you – she was covered with tan from a bottle, her face hidden by a large green cardboard sun hat. Christine – your wife, your partner – helped you to commit this crime, just as she helped you in the past when she "discovered" the body of Alice Corrigan at least twenty minutes before Alice Corrigan died – killed by her husband Edward Corrigan – you!'

Christine's voice was cold: 'Be careful, Patrick – don't lose your temper.'

Poirot said, 'The death of Nellie Parsons, also found strangled, may also be your work – I still have to prove this. But in the case of the Corrigan murder, both you and Christine were easily identified by the Surrey police from a group of people photographed here, while we were on our picnic. They identified you at once as Edward Corrigan, and you, Mrs Redfern, as Christine Deverill, the young woman who found the body.'

Patrick Redfern had got up. His handsome face was transformed. It was full of rage – the face of a killer.

'You interfering little worm!' he yelled at Poirot.

Patrick threw himself forward, his fingers stretching and curling, shouting, as he fastened his fingers round Hercule Poirot's throat...

CHAPTER 13

Poirot said thoughtfully, 'The morning we were sitting here that we talked of sunbathers lying so still they might be corpses, it was then I thought how little difference there was between them if you don't look closely. One young woman is very like another, when they just lie in the sun. There is no identity, no personality. It is when a woman walks, speaks, laughs, turns her head, moves a hand – then there is personality – then she is an individual.

'It was that day we spoke of evil under the sun. Mr Lane is very sensitive – he feels the presence of evil – but he did not know exactly where the evil was. To him, evil was focused in the person of Arlena Marshall.

'But to my mind, though evil was present, it was not in Arlena Marshall. I saw her always as a victim. Because she was beautiful, because men turned to look at her, it was assumed she was the type of woman who ruined lives. But I saw her very differently. She was the type of woman who men care for easily – and of whom they as easily become tired. And everything I found out about her made me believe this more.

'The first thing mentioned about her was how the man in whose divorce case she had been named, refused to marry her. It was then that Captain Marshall asked her to marry him. To a shy man like Captain Marshall, a public <u>ordeal</u> would be awful – that explains his love and pity for his first wife who was tried for a murder she had not committed.

'After her death another beautiful woman is being publicly <u>shamed</u>. Again, Marshall performs a rescue act. But this time he does not find very much to keep the relationship going. Arlena is stupid – she does not deserve his sympathy and protection. Yet though he becomes annoyed by her, he continues to feel sorry for her. She is, to him, like a child who cannot get further than a certain page in the Book of Life.

'With her passion for men, I saw that Arlena Marshall was prey for a certain type of man. In Patrick Redfern, with his good looks and his charm, I recognized that type. The man who makes his living, one way or another, out of women. Watching from my place on the beach, I was certain that Arlena was Patrick's victim, not the other way around.

'Arlena had recently received a large amount of money. It was left to her by an elderly admirer who had died. Now, she was the type of woman who is always tricked out of her money by some man or other. So it was perhaps unfortunate that she suddenly had quite a lot. Miss Brewster mentioned a young man who had been "ruined" by Arlena, but a letter from him which was found in her room, in fact said that she had given him money when *he* was in trouble, and not the other way around.

'And so, I have no doubt that Patrick Redfern also found it easy to get her to hand him large sums of money from time to time "for investment". He probably told her stories of great opportunities – how he would make a fortune for them both. That type of man usually escapes with all the money. If, however, Captain Marshall had found out what had happened to his wife's fortune, Patrick Redfern might have been in trouble.

'That did not worry him, however, because he was going to kill her when it became necessary. He had already got away with one murder – that of a young woman called Corrigan, whom he had married.

'In all his plans for each murder, he was helped by the woman who pretended to be his wife here, and to whom he was genuinely attached. A young woman as different from his victims as you could imagine – cool, calm, but loyal to him and a clever actress. Here with us, Christine Redfern acted the role of the "poor little wife" – intelligent rather than athletic. Think of the points she made, one after another. That she went red in the sun, her white skin, that heights made her feel dizzy – stories of getting stuck on Milan Cathedral. Nearly everyone spoke of her as a "little woman". She was in fact as tall as Arlena Marshall, but with very small hands and feet. She spoke of herself as a former schoolteacher, which emphasized an impression of intelligence. She never told us what she taught. It is true, she had worked in a school, but she was in fact a P.E. teacher. She was an active young woman who could climb like a cat and run like an athlete.

'The crime itself was perfectly planned. It was, as I mentioned, a very slick crime. The timing was perfect.

'And so let us examine the day of the crime. It was a fine day – this was essential. Patrick Redfern's first act was to go out very early – by the upstairs door from the bedroom corridor. Under his bathrobe he hid a green hat, exactly the same as the one Arlena was in the habit of wearing. He went across the island, down the ladder to Pixy Cove, and put it behind some rocks. Part One of the plan was complete.

'On the previous evening he had arranged to meet Arlena at Pixy Cove. If she heard anyone descending the ladder, or a boat came in sight, she was to hide inside Pixy's Cave, the secret of which he had told her, and wait there. That was Part Two.

'In the meantime, Christine went to Linda's room when she judged Linda would have gone for her early morning swim. She altered Linda's watch, putting it forward twenty minutes. There was, of course, a risk that Linda might notice her watch was wrong, but it did not matter. Christine's real alibi was the small size of her hands, which made it impossible for her to have committed the crime. Nevertheless, a second alibi was desirable.

Then in Linda's room she noticed the book on death rituals, open at a certain page. And when Linda came in and dropped a parcel of candles she realized what was in Linda's mind. It opened up some new ideas to her. The original idea had been to make everyone suspect Kenneth Marshall, by leaving a bit of his broken tobacco pipe underneath the Pixy Cove ladder.

'On Linda's return, Christine arranged for them to go to Gull Cove. She then returned to her own room, took out a bottle of artificial suntan from a locked suitcase, applied it carefully and threw the empty bottle out of the window where it just missed Emily Brewster who was swimming. Part Three of the plan was successfully completed.

'Christine then dressed in a white swimsuit. Over it she wore a big pair of beach trousers and a shirt with long, wide sleeves, all of which hid her new suntan.

'At quarter past ten, Arlena leaves for her meeting. Christine's task is easy. Keeping her own watch hidden, she asks Linda at twenty-five past eleven what the time is. Linda looks at her watch and replies that it is quarter to twelve. She then goes down to the sea and Christine packs up her painting things. As soon as Linda's not looking, Christine picks up the girl's watch, which she has taken off before going into the sea, and changes it back to the correct time. Then she hurries up the cliff path, runs across the narrow bit of land to the top of the ladder, takes off her baggy clothes and puts them and her painting box behind a rock. Then she goes quickly down the ladder.

'Arlena is on the beach below, wondering why Patrick is taking so long to arrive. She sees someone on the ladder – how annoying, it's Patrick's wife! She hurries into Pixy's Cave.

'Christine takes the hat from its hiding place, a false red curl pinned at the back of it, and lies down with the hat and curl covering her face and neck. The timing is perfect. A minute or two later, Patrick and Emily Brewster's boat comes around the coast. Remember, it is Patrick who bends down and examines the body, Patrick who is shocked by the death of his lady love! His witness has been carefully chosen. Miss Brewster does not like heights, so she will not attempt to go up the ladder. She will leave the cove by boat, Patrick naturally being the one to remain with the body – "in case the murderer may still be nearby".

'Miss Brewster rows off to fetch the police. As soon as the boat has disappeared, Christine jumps up, cuts the hat into pieces with the scissors Patrick has brought, stuffs them into her swimsuit and runs up the ladder. She gets back into her clothes and runs back to the hotel. There is just time to have a quick bath, washing off the brown suntan, and get into her tennis dress. But she does one other thing too – she burns the pieces of the green cardboard hat and the red hair in Linda's grate. As she suspected, Linda has been experimenting with a ritual using the wax and the pin.

'Then she goes down to the tennis court in time for 12 o'clock. She arrives last, but shows no signs that she has been hurrying.

'And, meanwhile, Patrick has gone to the cave. Arlena has seen nothing and heard very little – a boat, and some voices – but she has remained hidden. But now it is Patrick calling. '"All clear, darling," and she comes out, and his hands fasten round her neck – and that is the end of poor, foolish, beautiful Arlena Marshall…'

His voice died away.

For a moment there was silence, then Rosamund Darnley said with a shiver, 'But why did Linda imagine that she had actually killed Arlena?'

'Remember, she is little more than a child,' Poirot answered. 'She read that book and half-believed it. She hated Arlena. She made the wax doll, stabbed it in the heart, melted it away – and on that very day, Arlena dies. Older and wiser people than Linda have believed in sillier things. This unhappy girl believed she had killed her stepmother.'

Rosamund cried, 'Oh, poor child, poor child. And I thought something different – that she knew something which would—'

Rosamund stopped.

Poirot said, 'I know what it was you thought. You thought she knew her father, Captain Marshall, had killed Arlena. And your manner frightened Linda still further. She believed her action had really brought about Arlena's death and that you knew it. Christine Redfern worked on her too, introducing the idea of the sleeping tablets to her, showing her a quick end to the guilt of her crime. You see, once Captain Marshall was proved to have an alibi, it was vital for a new suspect to be found. Christine Redfern decided it would be Linda.'

Rosamund said, 'What a monster!'

Poirot nodded: 'A cold and cruel woman.'

◆ ◆ ◆

It had taken some days but Linda Marshall had recovered – at least her physical strength had returned. Now she sat with Hercule Poirot on Gull Cove.

'Of course, I'm glad I didn't die,' she was saying, 'but you know, Monsieur Poirot, it's just the same as if I'd killed her, isn't it? I meant to.'

Poirot said, 'It is not the same thing. The wish to kill and the action of killing are two different things. If, instead of a little wax figure in your bedroom, you had had your stepmother tied and helpless and a knife in your hand instead of a pin, you would not have pushed it into her heart! Something inside you would have said "no". It is the same with me. I get angry at a fool. I say, "I would like to kick him." Instead, I kick the table. And then, if I have not hurt my toe too much, I feel much better and the table is not usually damaged. To make the wax figures and stick in the pins did something useful for you – you took the hate out of yourself and put it into that little figure. And with the pin and the fire you destroyed – not your stepmother – but the hate you felt for her. Afterwards, before you heard about her death, you felt better, did you not? Happier?'

Linda nodded: 'How did you know? That's exactly how I felt.'

Poirot said, 'Then make up your mind not to hate your next stepmother.'

Linda was surprised, 'Do you think I'm going to have another? Oh, I see – you mean Rosamund. I don't mind her.' She hesitated a minute. 'She's sensible.'

It was not the adjective that Poirot himself would have selected for Rosamund Darnley, but he realized that it was Linda's idea of high praise.

◆ ◆ ◆

Kenneth Marshall and Rosumand were talking on the terrace.

'Rosamund,' said Kenneth gently, 'Did you get some extraordinary idea into your head that I'd killed Arlena?'

Rosamund looked rather embarrassed. She said, 'I suppose I was a fool.'

'Of course you were.'

'Yes, but Ken, I never knew what you really felt about Arlena. I thought if you'd suddenly found out she was seeing Patrick

Redfern, you might have gone mad with rage. I've heard stories about you. You're usually very quiet but you can be rather frightening sometimes too, when you're angry.'

'So you thought I just took her by the throat and strangled her?' said Marshall.

'Well, yes. And your alibi didn't seem very strong. That's when I decided to make up that silly story about seeing you typing in your room. And when I heard you said you'd seen me look into the room – well, that made me sure you'd done it. That, and Linda's odd behaviour.'

Kenneth Marshall said with a sigh: 'Don't you realize that I said I'd seen you in the mirror in order to confirm your story? I— I thought *you* needed an alibi.'

Rosamund stared at him:

'You don't mean you thought *I* killed your wife?'

Now Kenneth Marshall looked embarrassed.

Rosamund said, 'What motive do you think I had to kill Arlena?'

He looked away.

Rosamund cried, 'Ken! You thought I killed her for you, did you? Or— did you think I killed her because I wanted you myself?'

'Not at all,' said Kenneth Marshall. 'But you know what you said that day – about Arlena being bad for Linda – and you... you seemed to care what happened to me too.'

Rosamund said, 'I've always cared about that.'

'I believe you have. You know, Rosamund – I can't usually talk about things – I'm not good at talking – but I'd like to get this clear. I didn't care for Arlena, and living with her was absolutely awful, but I did feel very sorry for her. She was such a fool – she just couldn't help it – and the men she fell for always let her down and treated her badly. I simply felt I couldn't be the one to give her the final push. I'd married her, and it was up to me to look after her as best I could.'

Rosamund said gently, 'It's all right, Ken. I understand now.'

Without looking at her, Kenneth Marshall carefully filled a pipe with tobacco. He mumbled, 'You're pretty good at understanding, Rosamund.'

A faint smile curved Rosamund's mouth. She said, 'Are you going to ask me to marry you now, Ken, or are you going to wait six months?'

Kenneth Marshall's pipe dropped from his lips and crashed onto the rocks below.

'Oh no! That's the second pipe I've lost down here. How did you know I'd decided six months was the proper time?'

'I suppose because it *is* the proper time. But I'd rather have something definite now, please. Because in the next six months you may come across some other poor female who needs rescuing instead of me.'

He laughed.

'You're going to be the poor female this time, Rosamund. You're going to come with me and live in the country.'

Rosamund said softly, 'Oh, my dear, I've wanted to live in the country with you all my life! Now – it's going to come true…'

◆ CHARACTER LIST ◆

Hercule Poirot: famous Belgian detective, living in London.

Mr Odell and Mrs Carrie Gardener: middle-aged American tourists, on holiday in England.

Miss Emily Brewster: strong athletic woman who likes rowing.

Major Barry: retired army officer who served in India.

Mr Stephen Lane: tall, energetic man of fifty.

Mrs Christine: former school teacher, married to Patrick Redfern.

Mr Patrick Redfern: Christine's husband. A young, attractive man.

Mrs Arlena Marshall (*also known by her unmarried name,* **Arlena Stuart**): former actress and a stunning woman – very attractive to men.

Captain Kenneth Marshall: Arlena's husband. A businessman in his forties.

Miss Rosamund Darnley: successful London dress designer.

Miss Linda Marshall: Kenneth's sixteen-year-old daughter by his first wife, and Arlena's stepdaughter.

Mr Horace Blatt: businessman who enjoys sailing.

Inspector Colgate: police officer.

Dr Neasdon: local doctor who also works as a doctor for the police.

Colonel Weston: local Chief Constable who has worked with Poirot before.

Mrs Castle: owner of the Jolly Roger Hotel.

Gladys Narracott: chambermaid at the Jolly Roger Hotel.

♦ Cultural notes ♦

1 Devon
An area in south-west England. Devon is a popular place for tourists to visit, especially in summer. It offers many things for visitors to see and do, such as walking, sailing and enjoying the beautiful countryside.

2 Map of the island
See page vi for a map of the island.

3 Military titles
Different positions and jobs in the army, navy or air force have different titles. In *Evil Under the Sun*, Major Barry, Captain Marshall and Colonel Weston have military titles. **Colonel** ranks the highest of the three, and **Major** ranks higher than **Captain**.

4 Mussolini
Italian political leader from 1922 to 1943. Joined forces with Germany and Japan in the Second World War.

5 Princess Elizabeth
Now Queen Elizabeth II of the United Kingdom.

6 Women in society
In the time when *Evil Under the Sun* was written (1941), it was not yet common for women in the UK to have jobs outside of the house. Most women expected to get married and stay at home raising children. Businesswomen such as Rosamund Darnley were seen as unusual, and often looked up to.

Things would begin to change towards the end of the Second World War, when it became more common for women to have a jobs.

7 Non-military titles

In 1941, when *Evil Under the Sun* was published, Britain had a class system with rules that everybody knew and most people followed. People were either upper, middle or working class. Anyone with **Lord** or **Lady** in front of their name was from the upper classes.

The title **Sir** for a man is awarded to someone by the king or queen for something they have done for the country. This still happens today in the UK and the Commonwealth.

8 'Till death us do part'

This line is part of the traditional wedding vows. It means, 'We will stay together until one of us dies.'

9 Police titles

The structure of the police force and the ranks of the men and women who work there have not changed much since the Metropolitan Police was created in London in 1928. The ranks, starting at the lowest, are: Police Constable, Sergeant, Inspector, Chief Inspector, Superintendent, Chief Superintendent.

Throughout the country there is a structure of separate but co-operating police forces. Each one has a **Chief Constable** in charge. The Chief Constable does not usually participate in police operations but is more of a manager who makes important decisions. In this story, however, the Chief Constable, Colonel Weston, becomes actively involved in the case.

10 Hanging: the death penalty

When *Evil Under the Sun* was first published in 1941, the consequences of murder were different from today. If you killed a person on purpose, you could be punished for the crime by death. This was called the death penalty or a death sentence. Most people who were executed for these crimes were hanged by a rope tied around their necks.

The government ended the death penalty for murder in the UK in 1965.

11 Bridge

Bridge is a card game played by four players in two teams of two. It was an incredibly popular after dinner game when *Evil Under the Sun* was written.

12 Death Cults, Barbarian Rituals and Untraceable Poisons

This book that Poirot finds in Linda Marshall's room is about ways to bring about someone's death. Poirot finds it strange and worrying that Linda has such a book.

13 Scotland Yard

The headquarters of the British police in London. Scotland Yard was thought to have the best police force in the UK. They would often take over cases if they became too serious for the local police to handle, or whenever the case involved crimes in more than one area.

Scotland Yard (now New Scotland Yard) still exists in the UK today.

◆ Glossary ◆

abruptly ADVERB
If someone says something **abruptly**, they say it in a rude and unfriendly way.

acquit TRANSITIVE VERB
If someone **is acquitted** of a crime, it is formally declared in court that they did not commit it.

admirer COUNTABLE NOUN
A person's **admirer** is someone who likes and respects them.

adore TRANSITIVE VERB
If you **adore** someone, you love and admire them.

agonized ADJECTIVE
Agonized describes something that you say or do when you are in great physical or mental pain.

alibi COUNTABLE NOUN
If you have an **alibi**, you can prove that you were somewhere else when a crime was committed.

angle COUNTABLE NOUN
An **angle** is the shape that is created where two lines or objects join together.

arsenic UNCOUNTABLE NOUN
Arsenic is a very strong poison which can kill people.

awkward ADJECTIVE
If you feel **awkward**, you feel embarrassed and shy.

bathrobe COUNTABLE NOUN
A **bathrobe** is a loose piece of clothing made of the same material as towels. You wear it before or after you have a bath or a swim.

bitterly ADVERB
If you say something **bitterly**, you say it angrily or resentfully.

blackmail COUNTABLE NOUN
Blackmail is the action of threatening to reveal a secret about someone unless they do something you tell them to do, such as giving them money.
blackmailer COUNTABLE NOUN
A **blackmailer** is someone who uses blackmail against another person.

blind belief in someone PHRASE
If you have a **blind belief in someone**, you feel very certain that they are good or right without taking any notice of important facts about them.

bottled up PHRASAL VERB
If you describe someone as **bottled up**, you mean that they are tense and angry because they do not express or show their feelings. The usual expression is 'to keep things bottled up'.

brain TRANSITIVE VERB *(informal)*
To **brain** someone means to hit them forcefully on the head.

breach of promise PHRASE
If there is a **breach of promise**, you break a promise.

brute COUNTABLE NOUN
If you call a man a **brute**, you mean that he is rough and insensitive.

business UNCOUNTABLE NOUN
You can use **business** to refer in a general way to an event, situation, or activity. For example, you can say something is 'a distressing business' or you can refer to a situation generally as 'this whole business'.

cast-iron ADJECTIVE
A **cast-iron** alibi is absolutely certain to prove that someone was somewhere else when a crime was committed.

chambermaid COUNTABLE NOUN
A **chambermaid** is a woman who is employed to clean and tidy the bedrooms in a hotel.

cite TRANSITIVE VERB
To **cite** a person means to officially name them in a legal case.

composed ADJECTIVE
If you are **composed**, you are calm after being angry or excited.

contaminate TRANSITIVE VERB
If someone **is contaminated by** another person, they are damaged by that person.

copse COUNTABLE NOUN
A **copse** is a small group of trees growing very close to each other.

corpse COUNTABLE NOUN
A **corpse** is a dead body.

corroborate TRANSITIVE VERB
To **corroborate** something that has been said means to provide evidence that supports it.

cough up PHRASAL VERB *(informal)*
If you **cough up** money, you give someone money, usually when you would prefer not to.

cove COUNTABLE NOUN
A **cove** is a small bay on the coast.

current COUNTABLE NOUN
A **current** is a steady, continuous, flowing movement of water or air.

death ritual COUNTABLE NOUN
A **death ritual** is a type of ceremony based around death which involves a series of actions performed in a fixed order.

deck chair COUNTABLE NOUN
A **deck chair** is a simple chair with a folding frame, and a piece of canvas as the seat and back. Deck chairs are usually used on the beach, on a ship, or in the garden.

dining room COUNTABLE NOUN
The **dining room** is the room in a house or hotel where people have their meals.

diplomatic ADJECTIVE
Someone who is **diplomatic** is able to say or do things without offending people.

discretion UNCOUNTABLE NOUN
If something is done **at the discretion** of a person in a position of authority, they have the freedom and authority to decide what to do.

disgust UNCOUNTABLE NOUN
Disgust is a strong feeling of dislike or disapproval.

dressing table COUNTABLE NOUN
A **dressing table** is a small table in a bedroom with drawers and a mirror.

dubious ADJECTIVE
If you are **dubious** about something, you are unsure about it.

flamboyant ADJECTIVE
If you say that someone or something is **flamboyant**, you mean that they are very noticeable and stylish.

flaming ADJECTIVE
If someone has a **flaming** temper, they have a very bad temper.

float COUNTABLE NOUN
A **float** is a light object that is used to help someone or something float in water.

footstep COUNTABLE NOUN
A **footstep** is the sound made by someone's feet touching the ground when they are walking or running.

forgery COUNTABLE NOUN
You can refer to a fake banknote, document, or painting as a **forgery**.

get rid of PHRASE
If you **get rid of** someone or something, you make it/them leave or go away.

give you the shivers PHRASE
If someone or something **gives you the shivers**, they make you feel frightened or unhappy.

glittering ADJECTIVE
If something is **glittering**, it shines and sparkles.

go out of your way PHRASE
If you **go out of your way** to do something, you make a particular effort to do it.

gold-digger COUNTABLE NOUN
A **gold-digger** is a person who has a relationship with someone who is rich in order to get money or expensive things from them; used to show disapproval.

got it badly PHRASE
If you say that someone has **got it badly**, you mean that they find another person so attractive that they have fallen in love with them.

grate COUNTABLE NOUN
A **grate** is a framework of bars in a fireplace, which holds the coal or wood.

grudge COUNTABLE NOUN
If you have a **grudge** against someone, you have unfriendly feelings towards them because they have harmed you in the past.

gruff ADJECTIVE
A **gruff** voice sounds low and rough.

high tide UNCOUNTABLE NOUN
At the coast, **high tide** is the time when the sea is at its highest level because the tide is in.

hike COUNTABLE NOUN
If you go on a **hike**, you go for a long walk in the country.
hiker COUNTABLE NOUN
A **hiker** is someone who enjoys going on hikes.

hiss COUNTABLE NOUN
A **hiss** is a sound like a long 's'.

horrified ADJECTIVE
If someone looks **horrified**, they look shocked, disappointed, or disgusted.

imaginary ADJECTIVE
An **imaginary** person, place, or thing exists only in your mind or in a story, and not in real life.

inquest COUNTABLE NOUN
An **inquest** is an official inquiry into the cause of someone's death.

interfering ADJECTIVE
If you call someone **interfering**, you mean that they get involved in a situation although it does not concern them and their involvement is not wanted.

jealousy UNCOUNTABLE NOUN
Jealousy is a feeling of anger or bitterness because someone thinks that another person is trying to take a lover, friend, or possession, away from them.

knit INTRANSITIVE VERB
When someone **knits**, they make something from wool or a similar thread using knitting needles or a machine.

knitting UNCOUNTABLE NOUN
Knitting is something, such as an article of clothing, that is being knitted.
knitting needle COUNTABLE NOUN
Knitting needles are thin plastic or metal rods which you use when you are knitting.

ledge COUNTABLE NOUN
A **ledge** is a piece of rock on the side of a cliff or mountain, which is in the shape of a narrow shelf.

life and soul PHRASE
If you refer to someone as the **life and soul** of a place or event, you mean that they are very lively and entertaining, and are good at mixing with people.

linger INTRANSITIVE VERB
If you **linger** somewhere, you stay there for a longer time than is necessary.

loose end COUNTABLE NOUN
A **loose end** is part of a story or situation that has not yet been explained.

low tide UNCOUNTABLE NOUN
At the coast, **low tide** is the time when the sea is at its lowest level because the tide is out.

mainland SINGULAR NOUN
The **mainland** is the large main part of a country, in contrast to the islands around it.

man-eater COUNTABLE NOUN
(informal)
If a woman is described as a **man-eater**, she attracts many men, but does not always care about them; used to show disapproval.

mechanically ADVERB
If you say something **mechanically**, you say it automatically, without thinking.

mind is stronger than matter PHRASE
You can sometimes use the expression **mind is stronger than matter** to describe situations in which a person aims to control events or solve a physcial problem using their mind. The usual expression is 'mind over matter'.

mind your own business PHRASE
If someone **minds their own business**, they do not get involved in things that do not concern them personally.

modesty UNCOUNTABLE NOUN
Someone who shows **modesty** does not talk much about their abilities, achievements, or possessions; used to show approval.

monologue COUNTABLE NOUN
If you refer to a long speech by
one person during a conversation
as a **monologue**, you mean that
other people are not able to talk
or express their opinions.

murmur TRANSITIVE VERB
If you **murmur** something, you
speak very quietly, so that not
many people can hear what you
are saying.

narrow-minded ADJECTIVE
If you describe someone as
narrow-minded, you think they
are unwilling to consider new
ideas or other people's opinions;
used to show disapproval.

notorious ADJECTIVE
Someone or something that is
notorious is famous for
something bad.

obediently ADVERB
If someone does something
obediently, they do what they
are told to do.

old maid COUNTABLE NOUN
People sometimes refer to an old
or middle-aged woman as an **old
maid** when she has never married
and they think that it is unlikely
that she ever will marry. This
phrase can cause offence.

on the lookout PHRASE
If you are **on the lookout**, you
are watching out for something.

orchard COUNTABLE NOUN
An **orchard** is an area of land on
which fruit trees are grown.

ordeal COUNTABLE NOUN
An **ordeal** is an extremely
unpleasant and difficult
experience.

orderly ADJECTIVE
Something that is **orderly** is well
organized or well arranged.

panama hat COUNTABLE NOUN
A **panama hat** is a hat, worn
especially by men, that is woven
from the leaves of a palm-like
plant and worn when it is sunny.

pathetically ADVERB
If someone says something **pathetically**, they say it in a way that shows they are sad and weak or helpless, and they make you feel very sorry for them.

persist INTRANSITIVE VERB
If you **persist** in saying or doing something, you continue to say or do it, even though it may be difficult.

pipe COUNTABLE NOUN
A **pipe** is an object which is used for smoking tobacco.

prey UNCOUNTABLE NOUN
You can refer to the people who someone tries to harm or trick as their **prey**.

prosecute INTRANSITIVE VERB
If the authorities **prosecute**, they charge someone with a crime and put them on trial.

pulse COUNTABLE NOUN
Your **pulse** is the regular beating of blood through your body, which you can feel, for example, at your wrist or neck.

pyschiatric hospital COUNTABLE NOUN
A **psychiatric hospital** treats people who are suffering from mental illness.

reassuring ADJECTIVE
If you are **reassuring**, you say or do things to make someone stop worrying about something.

rouse TRANSITIVE VERB
If something **rouses** you, it makes you very emotional or excited.

scan TRANSITIVE VERB
When you **scan** an area, you look at it carefully, usually because you are looking for something in particular.

scented ADJECTIVE
If something is **scented**, it smells pleasant, often because it smells of perfume.

seasickness UNCOUNTABLE NOUN
If someone suffers from seasickness when they are travelling in a boat, they vomit or feel sick because of the way the boat is moving.

see red PHRASE
If you **see red**, you become very angry.

shady ADJECTIVE
Shady activities or people seem to be dishonest or illegal.

shame TRANSITIVE VERB
If somebody **is shamed**, someone or something causes them to feel shame.

sheer ADJECTIVE
A **sheer** cliff or drop is extremely steep or completely vertical.

silence TRANSITIVE VERB
To **silence** someone or something means to stop them speaking or making a noise.

siren COUNTABLE NOUN
Some people refer to a woman as a **siren** when they think that she is attractive but dangerous in some way.

slick ADJECTIVE
A **slick** action is done quickly and smoothly, and without any obvious effort.

smuggler COUNTABLE NOUN
A **smuggler** is a person who is involved in smuggling.
smuggling UNCOUNTABLE NOUN
Smuggling is the act of taking things or people into a place or out of it illegally or secretly.

stammer INTRANSITIVE VERB
If someone **stammers**, they speak with difficulty, hesitating and repeating words or sounds.

strangle TRANSITIVE VERB
To **strangle** someone means to kill them by tightly squeezing their throat.

strike down PHRASAL VERB
If someone **is struck down**, they are killed or severely harmed.

sue TRANSITIVE VERB
If you **sue** someone, you start a legal case against them to claim money from them because they have harmed you in some way.

sulky ADJECTIVE
If you are **sulky**, you are silent and bad-tempered for a while because you are annoyed.

suspect COUNTABLE NOUN
A **suspect** is a person whom the police think may be guilty of a crime.

sway INTRANSITIVE VERB
If someone **sways**, they lean or swing slowly from one side to the other.

try TRANSITIVE VERB
When a person **is tried**, they appear in court and are found innocent or guilty after the judge and jury have heard the evidence.

unreality UNCOUNTABLE NOUN
Unreality refers to a situation that it is so strange that you find it difficult to believe it is happening.

unsteadily ADVERB
If you do something **unsteadily**, you have difficulty doing it because you cannot completely control your body.

vamp COUNTABLE NOUN
If you describe a woman as a vamp, you mean that she uses her attractiveness to get what she wants; used to show disapproval.

wax UNCOUNTABLE NOUN
Wax is a solid, slightly shiny substance made of fat or oil which is used to make candles.

wickedness UNCOUNTABLE NOUN
Wickedness is used to talk about the quality of being very bad in a way that is deliberately harmful to people.

will COUNTABLE NOUN
A **will** is a legal document stating what you want to happen to your money and property after you die.

wink INTRANSITIVE VERB
If you **wink**, you look towards someone and close one eye very briefly, usually as a signal that something is a joke or a secret.